# The Book of Gingerbread

# The Book of Gingerbread

## 50 SPICED BAKES, HOUSES, COOKIES, DESSERTS & MORE

### Helena Garcia

Hardie Grant

QUADRILLE

# Contents

# Introduction

When I agreed to write this book and discussed it with friends and family, everyone's response was identical, 'I love gingerbread'. To this day I have not heard one person say the opposite.

After my first two very spooky books it may seem odd to write a book all about gingerbread, but I set out to do it differently. I purchased a few books on the subject and they all offered pretty much the same – gingerbread cookies and/or houses. I then decided to use gingerbread as a flavour for not just biscuits but for desserts like trifle or ice-cream, pies, donuts, cheesecakes etc. Ginger is such a beautiful and versatile ingredient that, paired up with treacle, butter and sugar, becomes a crowd-pleasing recipe that has endured the test of time.

I researched the history of gingerbread and unsurprising it used to be baked and bought as a treat – a celebratory bake that eventually would become synonymous with Christmas.

However, I could not write a recipe book without including some spooky twists along the way. In fact, spooky festive bakes are possibly my favourite to create so the subject of this book was the perfect excuse I needed to create more.

Gingerbread has not only inspired bakes, but it also plays a significant role in fairy tales and storytelling. From the gingerbread man to Hansel and Gretel, gingerbread goes beyond an edible treat, it is rooted in tradition.

I hope this book inspires you to use gingerbread in a variety of ways, for every day as well as for the festive season.

# A (VERY BRIEF)
## History of Gingerbread

*D*o you ever wonder why we eat the food we eat? Where does it come from and how did it end up on our plates?

One of the earliest recorded English gingerbread recipes from the fifteenth century doesn't actually contain any ginger but rather saffron, pepper, cinnamon and cloves. In those days, spices symbolized wealth, so making gingerbread was a way for a host to show off. Ginger (originally from China) was available at this time in Europe and by the late Middle Ages a more recognizable version of the gingerbread cookies we know today had been created.

The court of Queen Elizabeth I is the first documented location of a hard biscuit version of gingerbread. Presented as figures of queens and kings, the biscuits were shaped in hand-carved wooden moulds, then gilded with Dutch gold or an alloy of copper and zinc that imitated real gold leaf. Eating a decorated gingerbread soon became associated with food you would eat at fairs as a treat. These highly decorated biscuits became known as 'fairings' and eating them at a medieval fair would have brought you good luck.

It isn't surprising that in Victorian Britain gingerbread biscuits became a staple Christmas treat. By this point, gingerbread was already a food associated with celebration and special occasions. In Yorkshire, where I live, a sort of gingerbread cake called Pepper Cake was traditionally eaten at Christmas. The pepper in the cake was actually allspice, then referred to as 'Jamaican pepper'. It was also known as Carol Cake, as it was given to children in exchange for singing festive songs – this one in particular:

*A little bit of pepper-cake*
*A little bit of cheese*
*A little drink of water,*
*And a penny, if you please.*

The recipe for pepper cake is very similar to Yorkshire Parkin (see page 127), which is traditionally eaten on 5 November – Guy Fawkes Night or Bonfire Night. People here in Yorkshire still eat a slice of parkin with cheese. I cannot find a connection between pepper cake and Yorkshire parkin, but the fact that cheese is mentioned in the above rhyme makes me believe they are somehow connected.

Another sweet ginger treat associated with Christmas is, of course, the gingerbread house. Believed to have originated in Germany between the sixteenth and eighteenth centuries, the tradition of making them for Christmas must have spread to Britain during Victorian times. After the publication of *Hansel and Gretel* by the Brothers Grimm in 1812, the popularity of the gingerbread house rose dramatically, although in the original story the house is actually made of bread, the roof of cake and the windows of clear sugar.

In the book *The Truth About Hansel and Gretel* (*Die Wahrheit über Hänsel und Gretel*, 1963), German writer Hans Traxler claimed to have discovered the origins of the Brothers Grimm story. According to Traxler, the story dates back to the seventeenth century and Hansel and Gretel were in fact two adult bakers who murder the witch in order to steal her gingerbread recipe. The book provides an array of archaeological evidence, including the recipe. The German press, once again enchanted by the fairytale, picked up the story, which became national news and spread to foreign shores. None of it was true. It was, in fact, a literary prank and the ancient recipe turned out to be from a Dr. Oetker cookbook.

Gingerbread is not just something we eat, it has evoked fairy-tale stories, folklore and fantasy and is cemented in popular culture.

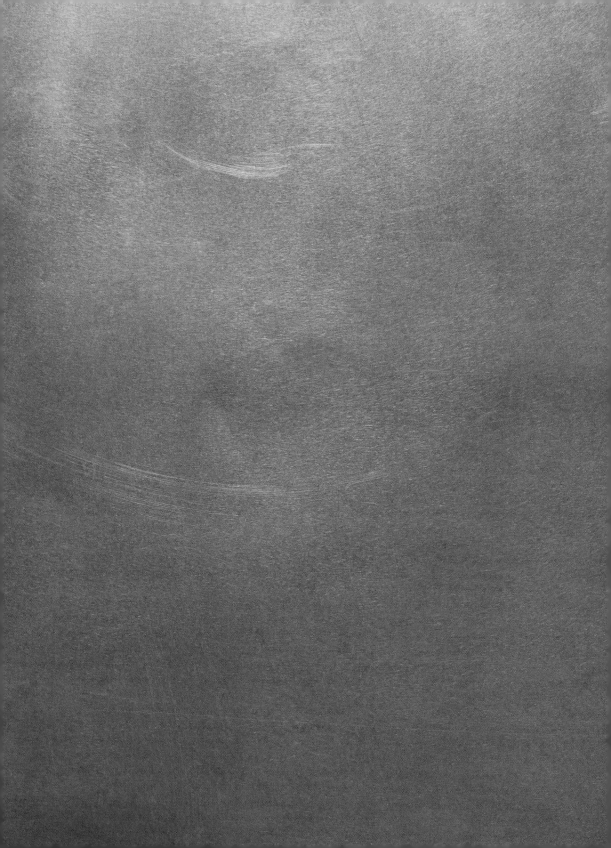

# Cakes and Bakes

# Gingerbread & Salted Caramel Cupcakes

150g (²/₃ cup) baking spread
150g (5oz/1 cup) demerara
 (light brown) sugar
3 large eggs
150g (5oz/1 cup plus 2 Tbsp)
 self-raising (self-rising) flour
1 tsp ground ginger
1½ tsp ground cinnamon
pinch of nutmeg
pinch of ground clove (optional)
65g (2¼oz/generous ½ cup)
 chopped pecans, plus a few
 extra for sprinkling

**FOR THE SALTED CARAMEL**
125g (4½oz/scant ²/₃ cup)
 granulated sugar
3 Tbsp water
115ml (3¾fl oz/scant ½ cup)
 double (heavy) cream
pinch of salt

**FOR THE BUTTERCREAM**
115g (½ cup) unsalted butter,
 at room temperature
300g (10½oz/2½ cups) icing
 (confectioners') sugar, sifted
1–2 Tbsp whole milk
1 tsp vanilla extract
¾ tsp ground cinnamon

If you fancy a quick and easy recipe that looks the part, look no further. Ginger, cinnamon and nutmeg are the Holy Grail of this book, but these cupcakes have also got chopped pecans in the batter and a salted caramel drizzle.

~

Preheat the oven to 200°C (180°C fan/400°F/Gas mark 6) and line a 12-hole cupcake tray with paper cases.

In a stand mixer, cream the baking spread and sugar on medium-high speed until light and fluffy. Add the eggs, one at a time, making sure to scrape the sides and bottom of the bowl. Gradually add the flour and spices, and continue mixing until fully incorporated. Add the pecans and stir through without overmixing.

Fill the cupcake cases three-quarters full with the batter and bake for 15–20 minutes, or until a toothpick inserted in the middle of the cupcakes comes out clean. Leave to cool on a wire rack.

For the salted caramel, combine the sugar and water in a small saucepan over a low-medium heat, swirling it until the sugar has dissolved. Turn the heat up and once the sugar starts to caramelize, remove the pan from the heat and add the cream in one go while stirring with a whisk. The caramel will bubble up, so be careful. Put the pan back on the heat and continue stirring while adding the salt. Let it cool.

To make the buttercream, in a large bowl, beat the butter with an electric mixer on medium speed until light and fluffy. Slowly add the icing sugar, milk, vanilla and cinnamon until fully combined. Add more milk if the mixture is too dry, or more icing sugar if too runny.

Scoop the buttercream into a piping bag fitted with a star nozzle and pipe on top of the cupcakes. Drizzle over a little salted caramel with a teaspoon and sprinkle with chopped pecans.

# Gingerbread Millionaire Shortbread

**FOR THE BISCUIT BASE**
200g (¾ cup plus 2 Tbsp)
  unsalted butter, at room
  temperature
100g (3½oz/½ cup) caster
  (superfine) sugar
250g (9oz/1¾ cups plus 2 Tbsp)
  plain (all-purpose) flour
2 tsp ground ginger
1 tsp ground cinnamon
¾ tsp freshly grated nutmeg

**FOR THE SALTED CARAMEL**
250g (9oz/1¼ cups) granulated
  sugar
6 Tbsp water
230ml (7¾fl oz/1 cup) double
  (heavy) cream
pinch of salt

**FOR THE CHOCOLATE TOPPINGS**
200g (7oz) milk or dark
  chocolate, chopped
50g (1¾oz) green candy melts
50g (1¾oz) white chocolate
edible glitter or sprinkles

When it comes to traybakes, millionaire shortbread is up there for me. Buttery biscuit base, topped with salted caramel and chocolate, what's there NOT to love?! To give this classic bake a twist, the base is made of ginger shortbread, and for a holiday finish I have added a winter wonderland scene on top made of chocolate, which is entirely optional.

Preheat the oven to 180°C (160°C fan/350°F/Gas mark 4) and line a 23-cm (9-in) square baking tin with baking paper.

In a stand mixer, beat the butter and sugar on medium-high speed until light and fluffy. Turn the speed down and add the flour, ginger, cinnamon and nutmeg, and continue mixing until everything is combined. The mixture will resemble breadcrumbs. Press the dough into the bottom of your prepared baking tin and bake for 20–25 minutes, or until golden brown. Leave to cool.

For the salted caramel, combine the sugar and water in a small saucepan over a low-medium heat, swirling it until the sugar has dissolved. Turn the heat up and, once the sugar starts to caramelize, remove the pan from the heat and add the cream in one go while stirring with a whisk. The caramel will bubble up, so be careful. Put the pan back on the heat and continue stirring while adding the salt. Pour the salted caramel on top of the biscuit layer and chill in the refrigerator for about 1 hour until set.

Melt the milk or dark chocolate in the microwave at 30-second intervals, then pour over the caramel. Smooth it out with an offset spatula. Chill in the refrigerator until the chocolate has hardened.

Meanwhile, make the chocolate decorations. You can choose whatever you like here – I went for a winter wonderland scene. Melt the green candy melts and pour into tree-shaped silicon moulds. Do the same with the white chocolate for the snowflakes, moon, and clouds. Attach all the decorations to the shortbread with a little melted chocolate and sprinkle with glitter or other decorative sprinkles.

# Gingerbread Cinnamon Roll Wreath

**FOR THE DOUGH**

265ml (9¼fl oz/generous 1 cup) whole milk, lukewarm

1 x 7-g (³⁄₁₆-oz) sachet of fast-action dried (active dry) yeast

55g (¼ cup) unsalted butter, melted

50g (1¾oz/¼ cup) caster (superfine) sugar

1 large egg, plus 1 egg yolk

480g (17oz/3½ cups) strong white bread flour, sifted, plus extra for dusting

½ tsp salt

**FOR THE FILLING**

55g (¼ cup) unsalted butter, melted

110g (4oz/½ cup) dark brown sugar

3 Tbsp maple syrup

2 tsp ground ginger

2 tsp ground cinnamon

¼ tsp freshly grated nutmeg

**FOR THE CREAM CHEESE FROSTING**

50g (¼ cup) unsalted butter, at room temperature

50g (1¾oz/½ cup) icing (confectioners') sugar, sifted

100g (3½oz/scant ½ cup) cream cheese, at room temperature

milk, as needed

**TO DECORATE**

handful of cranberries

holly leaves and ribbon

I love cinnamon rolls for breakfast and these ones are simply made for the perfect Christmas-morning treat. Prepare them the night before and leave to rise in the refrigerator overnight, then just bake in the morning and enjoy right after opening your presents.

Warm the milk in the microwave, then pour into a stand mixer fitted with the dough hook attachment. Sprinkle the yeast on top, add the melted butter, sugar, egg and egg yolk, followed by the flour.

Mix until everything is fully incorporated, then knead for 5 minutes. The dough will be a little sticky. Cover the bowl and leave it to rise for 1½ hours, or until doubled in size.

Tip the dough out onto a floured surface and roll out to a rectangle, 35 x 23cm (14 x 9in).

For the filling, mix together the butter, brown sugar, maple syrup and spices in a small bowl until fully incorporated. It spreads more easily if you warm it up in the microwave for 30 seconds. Spread the mixture over the dough, then tightly roll up the dough, starting from the short side. Place seam-side down and cut into 2.5cm (1in) rolls but only slice three-quarters of the way through, so they're still connected. Use kitchen scissors to snip the dough if it's easier. Form into a circle, so the cut sections fan outwards, and seal the ends. Line a baking tray with baking paper. Place the wreath on the tray and place a ramekin in the middle to help retain the centre hole. Cover and let it rise again for 45 minutes in a warm place, or leave in the refrigerator overnight. If left overnight, allow the rolls to come to room temperature before baking.

Preheat the oven to 195°C (175°C fan/375°F/Gas mark 5).

Bake for 20–25 minutes, or until golden brown.

Meanwhile, make the cream cheese frosting. Beat the butter until light and fluffy, then slowly add the icing sugar and keep mixing until you get a smooth consistency. Add the cream cheese and continue mixing until fully incorporated. If the mixture is too thick, loosen with a little milk.

Remove the wreath from the oven and allow to cool for 10 minutes. Drizzle with the cream cheese frosting and decorate with cranberries, holly leaves and a ribbon.

# Pumpkin, Maple & Ginger Cupcakes

215g (7½oz/1 cup) pumpkin purée
125g (4½oz/scant ⅔ cup) caster (superfine) sugar
100g (3½oz/½ cup) demerara (light brown) sugar
120ml (4fl oz/½ cup) vegetable oil
2 large eggs
180g (6¼oz/1⅓ cups) plain (all-purpose) flour
1 tsp baking powder
½ tsp bicarbonate of soda (baking soda)
½ tsp salt
1 tsp ground cinnamon
1 tsp ground ginger
½ tsp ground nutmeg
95g (3½oz/½ cup) candied chopped orange/lemon peel (or mixed peel)
95g (3½oz/½ cup) dried apricots
95g (3½oz/½ cup) prunes, chopped

**FOR THE MAPLE ICING**
170g (6oz/¾ cup) full-fat cream cheese, at room temperature
3 Tbsp unsalted butter, at room temperature
2 Tbsp maple syrup
400g (14oz/2 cups) icing (confectioners') sugar, sifted

crystallized ginger, to decorate

Pumpkin is not just an autumn fruit, it is very much a winter one too, and a perfect ingredient for sweet and savoury bakes. These cupcakes are a variation of the first bake I ever made in the *Bake Off* tent. It's sort of my version of a fruit cake because I think traditional fruitcakes are somewhat – how do I put this? – gross!

Preheat the oven to 200°C (180°C fan/400°F/Gas mark 6) and line a 12-hole muffin tin with 10 paper cupcake cases.

In a stand mixer fitted with the paddle attachment, mix the pumpkin purée, sugars and vegetable oil on medium speed. Add the eggs, one by one, mixing between each addition. Turn the speed to low and add the flour, baking powder, bicarbonate of soda, salt and spices. Continue mixing until all ingredients are fully incorporated, then add the chopped fruits and mix in by hand.

Fill the cupcake cases three-quarters full with the batter and bake for 20 minutes, or until a toothpick inserted in the middle comes out clean. Leave to cool completely on a wire rack.

Meanwhile, make the icing by mixing the cream cheese and butter in a stand mixer until light and creamy. Add the maple syrup and continue mixing. With the speed on low, slowly add the icing sugar until fully incorporated.

Spread the icing on top of the cooled cupcakes and sprinkle with the crystallized ginger.

# Gingerbread Present Brownies

170g (6oz) unsalted butter, at room temperature
130g (4½oz) dark chocolate, 70% cocoa solids
200g (7oz/1½ cups) plain (all-purpose) flour
4 Tbsp cocoa powder
1 tsp ground ginger
½ tsp ground cinnamon
½ tsp freshly grated nutmeg
½ tsp baking powder
½ tsp bicarbonate of soda (baking soda)
½ tsp salt
2 large eggs
200g (7oz/1 packed cup) demerara (light brown) sugar
80ml (2½fl oz/⅓ cup) treacle or molasses
1 tsp Ginger Syrup (page 123 or from a jar of stem ginger)

**FOR THE EGGNOG BUTTERCREAM**
4 Tbsp unsalted butter, at room temperature
115g (4oz/½ cup) cream cheese, at room temperature
1 tsp vanilla extract
260g (9oz/2¼ cups) icing (confectioners') sugar, sifted
¼ tsp ground nutmeg
2 Tbsp Eggnog (see page 102)

**TO DECORATE**
Christmassy sprinkles
50g (1¾oz) red fondant
50g (1¾oz) green fondant

Brownies always seem like an untouchable recipe for me – not only are they a staple of American baking, they're also a very difficult bake to decorate. I've faced my fears and done both, altering the classic recipe to include a touch of ginger and decorating them as presents with an eggnog icing. It's a simple way to elevate them – ideal for Christmas!

Preheat the oven to 180°C (160°C fan/350°F/Gas mark 4) and line a 23cm x 23cm (9 x 9in) brownie tin with baking paper.

Melt the butter and chocolate in a small saucepan over a low heat and set aside.

In a medium bowl, sift together the flour, cocoa powder, ginger, cinnamon, nutmeg, baking powder, bicarbonate of soda and salt. Set aside.

In a separate large bowl, whisk together the eggs, sugar, treacle and ginger syrup. Add the melted chocolate mixture and fold in, followed by the dry ingredients. Continue mixing until everything is just combined.

Pour the batter into your prepared tin and bake for 25–30 minutes. If you insert a toothpick to check consistency, brownies are best when slightly gooey on the inside. Leave to cool completely before turning out of the tin and decorating.

To make the buttercream, beat the butter and cream cheese in a stand mixer fitted with the paddle attachment or with a hand-held electric mixer on medium-high speed until light and fluffy. Add the vanilla and continue mixing. Turn the speed to low and add the icing sugar a little at a time, then add the nutmeg and finally the eggnog. Adjust the consistency, adding more icing sugar if it is too loose, or more eggnog if too dry.

Spread the eggnog buttercream over the brownies, sprinkle with your chosen sprinkles and cut them into squares. Make some ribbons and holly leaves out of fondant and use them to decorate the brownies as presents.

# Ginger & Chocolate Krampus Cupcakes

100g (3½oz/¾ cup) plain (all-purpose) flour
200g (7oz/1 cup) caster (superfine) sugar
45g (1½oz/⅓ cup) cocoa powder
¾ tsp ground ginger
1 tsp bicarbonate of soda (baking soda)
½ tsp baking powder
½ tsp salt
120ml (4fl oz/½ cup) buttermilk
60ml (2fl oz/¼ cup) vegetable oil
1 large egg
½ tsp vanilla extract
120ml (4fl oz/½ cup) freshly brewed coffee

**FOR THE BUTTERCREAM**
180g (6¼oz) dark chocolate, roughly chopped
250g (1 cup plus Tbsp) unsalted butter, at room temperature
1 extra large egg yolk
1 tsp vanilla extract
160g (5½oz/1¼ cup) icing (confectioners') sugar, sifted
3 tsp instant coffee powder
3 tsp Ginger Syrup (page 123 or from a jar of stem ginger) (optional)
black gel food colour

**TO DECORATE**
100g (3½oz) black fondant
100g (3½oz) red fondant
red lustre dust
clear piping gel

These cupcakes have an excellent flavour – rich and chocolatey with a hint of spice. Absolutely perfect. And to top it off, the frosting is good enough to eat on its own with a spoon. I reckon we could convince Krampus not to take us if we just gave him one of these cupcakes.

*elle*

Preheat the oven to 200°C (180°C fan/400°F/Gas mark 6) and line a 12-hole muffin tin with cupcake cases.

Sift the flour, sugar, cocoa powder, ginger, bicarbonate of soda, baking powder and salt into a large bowl. Mix with a whisk and set aside.

In a stand mixer fitted with the paddle attachment, mix the buttermilk, oil, egg and vanilla on medium speed. Turn the speed to low and add the dry ingredients and continue to mix. Slowly pour in the freshly brewed coffee and mix until everything is fully combined.

Fill the muffin cases to within 1cm (½in) of the top with the batter and bake for 15–20 minutes, or until a toothpick inserted in the middle comes out clean. Leave to cool completely before decorating.

To make the buttercream, put the chopped chocolate into a heatproof bowl and melt in the microwave at 30-second intervals. Set aside.

In a stand mixer fitted with the paddle attachment, beat the butter on medium-high speed until light and fluffy. Add the egg yolk and vanilla and continue mixing. Turn the speed to low and add the icing sugar, 1 tablespoon at a time, and continue to mix until it's all incorporated and the mixture is light and creamy. Dissolve the instant coffee powder in 1 teaspoon of hot water and add it to the mixture followed by the melted chocolate and ginger syrup, if using. Add enough gel colour to get a deep black shade. Transfer to a piping bag fitted with a large star nozzle and set aside until you are ready to decorate the cupcakes.

Make 24 goat's horns out of black fondant and 12 tongues out of red fondant. It helps to brush some red lustre dust on the edges of the tongues to give depth. Add some clear piping gel to each tongue for a wet look. Pipe a buttercream swirl on top of each cupcake and attach a pair of horns and a tongue to each.

# Santa Baby Ginger Swiss Roll

I find this recipe incredibly festive and fun. The green and red stripes on the cake make it Christmassy and the Santa pin-up legs add a little cheekiness. The sponge is vanilla and the ginger touch is in the cream cheese filling. It's a much lighter alternative to the sticky ginger cakes in this book.

*ellee*

Preheat the oven to 200°C (180°C fan/400°F/Gas mark 6). Lightly brush a 23 x 33cm (9 x 13in) baking tray (the kind you would use for a Swiss (jelly) roll) with vegetable oil and line neatly with baking paper.

Beat the eggs and sugar in a stand mixer or with a hand-held electric whisk for about 10 minutes to the ribbon stage (thick enough to make a ribbon shape with the whisk). Mix in the vanilla, then add half the flour and fold in carefully, ensuring you don't knock out too much air, until fully incorporated. Repeat with the remaining flour. Add 1 tablespoon of lukewarm water and fold in.

Divide the batter in half and colour one half red and the other green, carefully folding the food colour in until you get uniform colours. Pour the batters into separate piping bags, cut the ends and pipe alternating diagonal lines of batter into your prepared tin.

Bake in the centre of the oven for 10–12 minutes until just firm to the touch.

Meanwhile, make the filling. Beat the cream cheese and butter in a stand mixer on medium-high speed until smooth. Add the ginger juice and mix well, then reduce the speed to low and add the icing sugar, one spoonful at a time. When it has all been added, turn the mixer back to high speed and beat for a further 2 minutes until light and fluffy.

Lay out a damp dish towel on your work surface and place a piece of baking paper larger than the sponge on top. Remove the sponge from the oven and turn it out onto the prepared paper. Use the paper and dish towel to help you tightly roll the sponge up starting from a short edge, then leave it rolled up, paper inside, until cool. Unroll it and spread the cream cheese filling over the surface of the sponge, leaving a 2cm (¾in) gap at the edges on all sides. (Reserve the leftover filling, place in a piping bag fitted with a small star nozzle and set aside.) Roll the sponge back up and trim the edges, then wrap in clingfilm (plastic wrap) and refrigerate, seam-side down.

Make three pairs of legs out of the red fondant, shaping the feet and knees and bending one leg of each pair slightly. Insert a toothpick inside each leg to help place into the sponge. Let dry before you paint in the black boots with edible paint or pen. Pipe a little of the cream cheese filling at the top of each boot for a furry-looking finish (optional).

Remove the cake from the refrigerator and unwrap. Place it on a serving plate and pipe three swirls of the cream cheese filling on top. Add some sprinkles, if using, and press the Santa legs into the cream swirls.

vegetable oil, for greasing
3 large eggs
125g (4½oz/⅔ cup) caster (superfine) sugar
1 tsp vanilla extract
125g (4½oz/scant 1 cup) plain (all-purpose) flour, sifted
red gel food colour
green gel food colour

**FOR THE FILLING**
170g (6oz) full-fat cream cheese
85g (¾ cup) unsalted butter
1–1½ Tbsp ginger juice – made by grating and squeezing 1 large fresh ginger root through muslin (cheesecloth)
280g (10oz/2¼ cups) icing (confectioners') sugar, sifted

**TO DECORATE**
100g (3½oz) red fondant
toothpicks
black edible paint or pen
red and green sprinkles (optional)

# Ginger Spiced Banana Bread

100ml (3½fl oz/scant ½ cup) vegetable oil, plus extra for greasing
4 eggs
100g (3½oz/½ cup) caster (superfine) sugar
100g (3½oz/½ cup) dark brown sugar
150g (5oz/1 cup plus 2 Tbsp) plain (all-purpose) flour
1 tsp ground ginger
½ tsp ground cinnamon
½ tsp baking powder
1 tsp bicarbonate of soda (baking soda)
pinch of salt
4–5 medium bananas, mashed

**TO SERVE (OPTIONAL)**
whipped cream
Ginger Syrup (page 123 or from a jar of stem ginger)
freshly grated nutmeg

I find banana bread makes the perfect breakfast food. I'm Spanish and we tend to eat something sweet for breakfast. Banana bread ticks many boxes – it has fruit in it for a start. Adding a ginger-based spice mix makes this recipe a warming and nutritious snack for a chilly winter morning.

*ellee*

Preheat the oven to 200°C (180°C fan/400°F/Gas mark 6) and thoroughly grease a 900g (2lb/6 cup) loaf tin. I used a pumpkin-patterned one.

In a stand mixer fitted with the paddle attachment, mix the eggs, sugars and oil until combined. Add the flour, spices, baking powder, bicarbonate of soda and salt, and continue mixing. Add the mashed bananas and beat until just mixed in.

Pour the batter into your prepared tin and bake for 30–35 minutes.

Leave to cool in the tin for 5–10 minutes, then unmould. Serve sliced with whipped cream sweetened with ginger syrup and sprinkled with freshly grated nutmeg, if you like.

# Gingerbread, Pecan & Caramel Bundt

250g (1 cup plus 2 Tbsp) unsalted butter, plus extra for greasing
375g (13oz/generous 2¾ cups) plain (all-purpose) flour, plus extra for dusting
1 tsp baking powder
1 tsp bicarbonate of soda (baking soda)
½ tsp salt
4 Tbsp ground ginger
1 Tbsp ground cinnamon
½ tsp freshly grated nutmeg
250g (9oz/1¼ cups) demerara (light brown) sugar
120g (4¼oz/6 Tbsp) black treacle or molasses
300ml (10½fl oz/generous 1¼ cups) whole milk
3 large eggs
120g (4¼oz/1 cup) pecans, roughly chopped

**FOR THE SAUCE**
50g (3½ Tbsp) unsalted butter, cubed
180g (6¼oz/scant 1 cup) light muscovado sugar
1 Tbsp black treacle or molasses
pinch of salt
225ml (7½fl oz/scant 1 cup) double (heavy) cream

**TO DECORATE**
rosemary, thyme or pine sprigs, or a combination of all three
cranberries
candles (optional)

This is a delicious cross between the Gingerbread Candelabra Dome Cake (page 86) and the Sticky Toffee Gingerbread Pudding (page 95), with added pecans. It is also a perfect substitute for a Christmas pudding and a lot less work than the candelabra cake. Decorate with winter greens or herbs, such as pine sprigs or rosemary, sugared cranberries, star anise and orange slices, if you like. I kept mine simple.

*ellee*

Preheat the oven to 180°C (160°C fan/350°F/Gas mark 4). Butter and flour the inside of your 25cm (10in) bundt tin, or spray with non-stick baking spray.

Sift the flour, baking powder, bicarbonate of soda, salt and spices into a large bowl and set aside.

Melt the butter, sugar and treacle in a large saucepan over a low-medium heat, stirring constantly, until everything is combined. Slowly add the milk and warm through. Pour into the dry ingredients and mix until fully combined. Add the eggs, one by one, beating after each addition. Finally, mix in the pecans.

Pour the batter into your prepared tin and bake for 40–50 minutes, or until a skewer inserted in the middle comes out clean. Leave to cool in the tin for 5–10 minutes, then unmould.

To make the sauce, combine the butter, muscovado sugar, treacle and salt in a heavy-based saucepan over a low heat. Mix until everything is fully combined, then add the cream. Turn up the heat until it bubbles and thickens, and you get a nice toffee colour. Remove from the heat.

Pour the sauce over the cooled cake and decorate with wintery herbs or greens, sugared cranberries or star anise and sliced oranges – it's up to you. You can add candles before bringing to the table.

# Winter Spirit Candle Cake

A candle cake to guide us through the darkness of winter – and feed us, for that matter. The idea for this cake started with wanting to make a Christmas version of my Vampire Tears Candle Cake from my previous book, *The Wicked Baker*, but somehow developed into a wintery Green Man-style spirit sculpted into a candle. The flavours are staples of winter baking and go perfectly together – rich, sticky ginger sponge paired with a light, eggnog-flavoured Swiss meringue buttercream.

ᒥᐯᐟ

Preheat the oven to 200°C (180°C fan/400°F/Gas mark 6). Butter and flour three 10-cm (4-in) round cake tins. Alternatively, line a 23 x 33cm (9 x 13in) baking tray with baking paper.

Sift the flour, bicarbonate of soda, spices and salt into a large bowl and set aside.

Combine the butter, sugar, treacle, syrup and milk in a medium saucepan over a low-medium heat and stir until the sugar dissolves. Turn the heat up and bring the mixture to just before boiling point.

Pour the hot treacle mixture into the dry ingredients and mix with a spatula. Add the egg and continue mixing until everything is fully combined. Divide the batter between the prepared tins and bake for 20–25 minutes, or until a toothpick inserted in the middle comes out clean. Turn out onto a wire rack and leave to cool completely.

To make the Swiss meringue buttercream, place the egg whites and sugar into a heat-resistant bowl over a pan of simmering water, making sure the bottom of the bowl doesn't touch the water. Whisk the mixture constantly until the sugar is fully dissolved and you can no longer feel any granules between your fingers, or until the mixture reaches 60°C (140°F) on a sugar thermometer. Remove the bowl from the pan and transfer the mixture to a stand mixer fitted with the whisk attachment. Beat on high speed until light and fluffy – 10–15 minutes in total. Once you get glossy soft peaks, start adding the butter a cube at a time, letting the butter incorporate before adding the next piece. The mixture will deflate at first, but will fluff up again. Add the nutmeg and rum, and mix until combined.

Time to assemble the cakes. If you baked in a baking tray, cut out four circles of sponge with a 10cm (4in) cookie cutter. Layer some buttercream between each sponge layer and stack them up, finishing with a crumb coat of buttercream over the whole surface of the cake. Refrigerate the cake for half an hour and do a second coat of buttercream. If you have leftover buttercream, it freezes well so you can store it until you next need it.

Roll out the marzipan to 5mm (¼in) thick. Trim it to a rectangle with the short side measurng the exact height of your cake and long enough to cover the sides. Roll the marzipan around the cake and smooth, leaving the top uncovered. Sculpt the nose, eyes, eyebrows and mouth of the winter spirit out of the leftover marzipan and stick to the side of the cake. Cut out several leaves with cookie or fondant cutters and layer them all around the face.

Melt the white chocolate in the microwave in 30-second intervals and pour into a piping bag.

Place the birthday candle in the middle of the cake, but don't push it all the way in (this ensures you don't get a crack in the chocolate layer when you come to serve). Cover the top of the cake with the white chocolate and start creating the first layer of 'wax' drips by piping the chocolate around the edges of the cake. Refrigerate until the drips set, then repeat the process until you achieve the desired look.

When ready to serve, push the candle all the way into the cake and light before serving.

115 g (½ cup) unsalted butter, plus extra for greasing
225g (8oz/1¾ cups) self-raising (self-rising) flour, plus extra for dusting
1 tsp bicarbonate of soda (baking soda)
1 Tbsp ground ginger
1 tsp ground cinnamon
½ tsp freshly grated nutmeg
¼ tsp ground cloves
¼ tsp salt
115g (4oz/generous ½ cup) demerara (light brown) sugar
115g (4oz/6 Tbsp) black treacle or molasses
115g (4oz/6 Tbsp) golden syrup
250ml whole milk
1 egg

**FOR THE SWISS MERINGUE BUTTERCREAM**
75g (2½oz) egg white (about 2 egg whites)
115g (4oz/generous ½ cup) caster (superfine) sugar
250g (1 cup plus 2 Tbsp) unsalted butter, at room temperature, cubed
1 tsp freshly grated nutmeg
2 Tbsp rum

**TO DECORATE**
500g (1lb 2oz) white marzipan
200g (7oz) white chocolate, roughly chopped
1 birthday candle

# Focaccia Della Befana

520g (1lb 2½oz/3½ cups) strong white bread flour
120g (4¼oz/scant ⅔ cup) caster (superfine) sugar
1 x 7-g (³⁄₁₆-oz) sachet fast-action dried (active dry) yeast
100ml (3½fl oz/scant ½ cup) whole milk, lukewarm
100g (7 Tbsp) margarine, at room temperature
2 tsp salt
2 eggs, plus 1 yolk for brushing
1 Tbsp Ginger Syrup (page 123 or from a jar of stem ginger)
demerara (light brown) sugar, to decorate

**FOR THE FILLING**
200ml (7fl oz/1 cup) double (heavy) cream
2 Tbsp Ginger Syrup (page 123 or from a jar of stem ginger)

Have you ever heard of the Christmas witch? La Befana is a witch in Italian folklore who flies around on the eve of Epiphany delivering sweets and gifts to children who have been good and coal to those who have been naughty. On the day of Epiphany (6 January) in the Piedmont region, *focaccia della befana* – a sweet, enriched dough bake – is eaten. In Spain, children receive their presents from the Three Kings on this day and we eat kings' cake (*roscón de reyes*). This recipe is a fusion between the roscón and the focaccia with no candied fruit. Italian purists should look away now as I've given this traditional bread a ginger-flavoured cream filling.

*ellle*

Put the flour, sugar and yeast in a stand mixer fitted with a dough hook and start mixing on slow speed. Add the milk and continue mixing, then add the margarine, salt and whole eggs, one at a time. Finally, add the ginger syrup, increase the speed to medium-high and knead the dough for 10 minutes. Cover the bowl with a damp dish towel and let it rise in a warm place for 4–6 hours, or until it has tripled in size.

Knock the air out of the dough and place it in the middle of a baking tray lined with baking paper. Roll the dough out to a circle, 25cm (10in) in diameter. For the star shape, divide the dough into four quarters using a pizza cutter, without cutting all the way through the middle. Cut each quarter into four equal pieces, then twist each piece a number of times. To maintain the shape, encircle the dough with an unhinged springform cake tin (or you could bake it inside a 25cm (10in) cake tin). Cover the shaped focaccia with a damp dish towel and leave to rise for 1 hour.

Preheat the oven to 200°C (180°C fan/400°F/Gas mark 6). First glaze the dough with the egg yolk and sprinkle with some demerara sugar, then bake for 25 minutes, or until golden brown. Leave to cool completely.

Whip the cream and ginger syrup together, cut the focaccia in half and fill with the ginger cream before serving.

# Santa Claws Gingerbread Donuts

When it comes to donuts, you can fry them, you can bake them, but the most delicious type of all is the brioche donut. They require more effort for sure, but if you are going to do something, why not make the best version of it? The egg and butter make these donuts so much richer. To decorate, I've gone for a simple red glaze to represent Santa's coat and the nails are carved almonds.

Add the flour, yeast, sugar, spices and salt to a stand mixer fitted with a dough hook, making sure the yeast and salt don't touch at first. Mix on a low speed, then add the egg and egg yolk, butter and water, turn the speed up to medium and knead for about 10 minutes, or until the dough comes together. Cover the bowl with a damp dish towel and leave to rise in a warm place for 1–2 hours, or until doubled in size.

Line a baking tray with baking paper or a silicon mat.

Once the dough has doubled in size, punch it down and turn it out onto a lightly floured surface. Roll the dough into a log and cut into 8–10 equal pieces. Roll each piece into a ball and place on the prepared tray. Cover and leave to rise for another 30 minutes or so.

Heat a 5cm (2in) depth of oil in a large heavy-based pan over a medium heat to around 180°C (350°F), or until a breadcrumb added to the hot oil sizzles and browns in 30 seconds.

Before you start frying the donuts, cut three incisions, 2cm (¾in) long, into each piece to make the fingers of the paw. Fry 3 or 4 donuts at a time, depending on the size of your pan, on each side until golden brown. Remove with a slotted spoon to drain on paper towels and leave to cool.

To make the glaze, put the chopped chocolate into a heat-resistant bowl. Pour the double cream into a saucepan and bring to a simmer over a low-medium heat (do not let it boil), then pour the cream onto the chocolate and stir until fully melted. Add the food colour and stir again until fully incorporated.

Dip the tops of the donuts into the glaze, one by one, so the tops are red but the fingers are uncoated. Place on a wire rack until completely set.

To finish, carve the almonds into nail shapes and place one on each finger – you can make an incision first with a skewer so they go in easier, if you like. Pipe some shell shapes with buttercream or royal icing to imitate Santa's sleeve cuffs.

330g (11½oz/2½ cups) plain (all-purpose) flour, plus extra for dusting
½ x 7-g (¼-oz) sachet of fast-action dried (active dry) yeast
1½ Tbsp caster (superfine) sugar
½ tsp ground cinnamon
½ tsp ground ginger
½ tsp salt
1 large egg plus 1 egg yolk
55g (¼ cup) unsalted butter, at room temperature
120ml (4fl oz/½ cup) water
vegetable oil, for frying

**FOR THE GLAZE**
150g (5oz) white chocolate, roughly chopped
150ml (5fl oz/scant ⅔ cup) double (heavy) cream
red cocoa-based food colour

**TO DECORATE**
40 blanched whole almonds
Buttercream or royal icing (page 47) for the cuffs

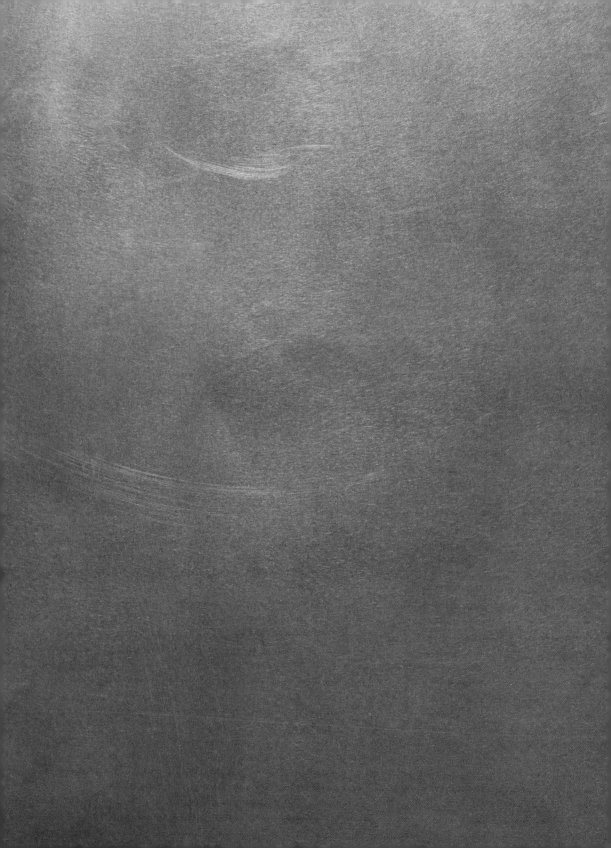

# Cookies

# Basic Gingerbread Dough

350g (12oz/2⅔ cups) plain
  (all-purpose) flour, plus extra
  for rolling out
1 tsp bicarbonate of soda
  (baking soda)
2 tsp ground ginger
1 tsp ground cinnamon
¼ tsp ground cloves
¼ tsp salt
125g (9 Tbsp) unsalted butter,
  at room temperature
175g (6oz/generous ¾ cup)
  brown sugar
1 free-range egg
4 tbsp golden syrup or molasses

This is my go-to gingerbread recipe for shaped cookies and houses. It will give you enough dough to make around 20 average-size gingerbread men. I always make gingerbread dough by hand in a ceramic bowl with a wooden spoon. You can, of course, use an electric mixer, but there's something so wonderfully rustic about gingerbread that it makes me want to work harder.

In a large bowl, sift together the flour, bicarbonate of soda, spices and salt. Set aside.

Add the butter and sugar to a stand mixer fitted with the paddle attachment and beat until well mixed (alternatively, mix by hand in a bowl, with a wooden spoon). Add the egg and golden syrup or molasses, then add the flour mixture and continue mixing just to bring it together.

Tip the dough out onto the work surface and knead slightly until smooth, then wrap in clingfilm (plastic wrap) and chill in the refrigerator for 30 minutes.

## To Bake
Preheat the oven to 180°C (160°C fan/350°F/Gas mark 4) and line two baking trays with baking paper.

Roll out the dough on a lightly floured surface to about 5mm (¼in) thick. Cut out your desired shapes and place on the prepared baking trays, spacing them at least 5cm (2in) apart.

Bake for 12–15 minutes, or until golden brown. Leave to cool on a wire rack. Store in an airtight container for 2–3 weeks.

# Royal Icing

3 large egg whites
550g (1lb 4oz/4 cups) icing
(confectioners') sugar, sifted
1 tsp vanilla extract
½ tsp salt

**There is no making gingerbread men without the need for royal icing. This is a no-fail recipe for it.**

In a stand mixer fitted with the whisk attachment, beat the egg whites until frothy. Add the icing sugar, 1 tablespoon at a time, until fully incorporated. Add the vanilla extract and salt, then mix until smooth. You are looking for a pipeable consistency. If the consistency is too runny, add a bit more icing sugar – a little at a time. If it's too thick, add a little water – again, just a little at a time until you have reached the desired pipeable consistency. Fresh royal icing will need to be used within 3 days and stored in the refrigerator, or you can freeze it for up to 3 months.

# Traditional (sort of) Gingerbread Men

1 x batch Basic Gingerbread
  Dough (page 46)

**TO DECORATE**
1 x batch Royal Icing (page 47)
black lustre dust
green gel food colour
red gel food colour
pink food colour
100g (3½oz) white fondant
50g (1¾oz) red fondant
red, orange and yellow isomalt
  or hard candy sweets
  (optional)

There are endless possibilities when it comes to the gingerbread man. There's absolutely nothing wrong with the traditional one, but I think it's fun to represent each year with a gingerbread person/creature inspired by its events. The key to making it work is to keep the traditional gingerbread man shape and some of its characteristics in place, like the buttons.

For example, in Christmas 2020, I made a Covid Gingerbread Man with a piped face mask and Covid virus buttons; Christmas 2022 was a gingerbread Queen and corgi to commemorate Elizabeth II's Platinum Jubilee; and the year *Stranger Things* came out I made a gingerbread demogorgon (which you can find on page 54).

These traditional gingerbread men are inspired by the ones in the 2015 film, *Krampus*. Their pointy candy canes are made with fondant for ease, but if you're brave with sugar work you can go for it. I made one of them leaping out covered in flames of isomalt just for fun.

ᘉᘉ

Make the gingerbread dough according to the instructions on page 46.

After rolling the dough, cut out 10 gingerbread men shapes and use the offcuts of dough to shape some frowny eyebrows for each character.

Bake according to the instructions on page 46. As soon as you take them out of the oven, while still warm, shape the inside of the mouths with a ball modelling tool. Let the gingerbread men cool completely on a wire rack before decorating.

Paint the inside of the mouth with the black lustre dust.

Divide the royal icing and colour some in green for the pupils of the eyes and red for the mouths. Pop into individual pipings bags and have fun drawing in the demonic details! But don't forget the pink cheeks. Use the

PLEASE
TURN OVER ☛

50

white royal icing to pipe the buttons, zig-zags for the hands and feet and the foaming mouth.

To make the pointy candy cakes, form the white fondant into a 20cm (8in) log. Divide the red fondant in half and form into two log shapes the same length as the white one. Form into a single log with a stripe of red on each side of the white. On the worktop, use your hands to roll out the log (without twisting at this stage) to the desired thickness you want the candy canes to be. Next, roll each end of the log in opposite directions with your fingertips, working along its length, to create the red and white twist effect. Cut into 15cm (6in) pieces, then curve one end and roll the other end to a sharp point for each cane. Allow them to dry out on a tray.

If you choose to make the isomalt flames, melt the red, orange and yellow isomalt in three separate bowls following the packet instructions. Pour blobs of red isomalt onto a silicon mat, add smaller blobs of orange on top and yellow above, then shape into flame-like shapes with a toothpick. Alternatively, melt yellow and red hard candies in the oven on a silicon mat and carefully shape in the same way while hot. Attach the flames to the gingerbread men with blobs of royal icing.

# Gingerbread Demogorgon

1 x batch Basic Gingerbread
  Dough (page 46)
250g (9oz) red fondant or
  modelling chocolate
red and black lustre dust
1 x batch Royal Icing (page 47),
  uncoloured
50g (1¾oz) black fondant

**To make your own demogorgon template, draw the shape of a gingerbread man on a piece of baking paper, shaping the head like five spreading flower petals and give the hands bent fingers, then cut it out. I have included my own template I drew at the end of this book (see page 144) if you'd rather go with that one.**

*eOle*

Make the gingerbread dough according to the instructions on page 46.

After rolling the dough out, use your template to cut out your demogorgon shapes, cutting around the baking paper with a sharp knife, and place on a baking tray lined with baking paper. Cover the finger areas with pieces of foil as they are likely to burn due to their delicate shape.

Bake according to the instructions on page 46, then let them cool completely on a wire rack before decorating.

Roll out the red fondant or modelling chocolate to 3mm (⅛in) thick. Use the head of the demogorgon template to cut out the petal shapes. Brush a little water on the back of the fondant shape to help it stick to the cookie. Make a hole in the middle of the fondant-covered head using a ball modelling tool, then lift the edges of the hole and paint the inside with black lustre dust. Paint the edges and the middle of each petal shape with red lustre dust to create depth and definition. Pipe the teeth with uncoloured royal icing.

To make the *Stranger Things*-inspired buttons, roll the black fondant with an offcut of the red fondant that is about a third of its size into a log shape. Marble the two colours together by bending the log in half and rolling it again a couple of times. Break off little pieces of the marbled fondant and roll them into small balls. Attach them to the demogorgon using a little royal icing.

## Eat before it eats you!

# Gingerbread & Eggnog SandWitch Cookies

1 x batch Basic Gingerbread
   Dough (page 46)
black lustre dust (optional)

**FOR THE EGGNOG FILLING**
100g (7 Tbsp) unsalted butter
5 Tbsp Eggnog (page 102)
dash of rum or brandy
   (optional)
freshly grated nutmeg
375g (3 cups) icing
   (confectioners') sugar, sifted

Did you ever hear the tale of the Christmas Witch? In Italy, La Befana is an old witch who delivers gifts to children on the night of 5 January (the eve of Epiphany). She is often represented flying on her broomstick covered in soot, since she enters children's homes through the chimney like Santa Claus. These cookies are inspired by La Befana and they're a holiday delight, just like her.

*ellee*

Make the gingerbread dough according to the instructions on page 46.

After rolling the dough, use a small flying witch cookie cutter to stamp a shallow impression, then use a round cutter to cut around each one, to make 20–24 witch-stamped circles. I use a round cookie cutter, 7cm (2¾in) in diameter, because my flying witch shape fits just right inside it. Place your stamped cookies on a baking tray lined with baking paper.

Bake according to the instructions on page 46, then let them cool completely on a wire rack before decorating.

Paint in the witch silhouette with the black lustre dust. It helps to use the witch cutter here, placing it on the cookie and painting inside the shape, so you don't go over the lines.

To make the eggnog filling, combine the butter, eggnog and dash of rum or brandy (if using) in a medium saucepan and bring to the boil over a low-medium heat. Remove from the heat and let it cool slightly, then whisk in the nutmeg and icing sugar until you get a spreadable consistency (you may not need all of the sugar). It will thicken further when fully cooled. If it hardens too much before you use it, just reheat it a little.

Spread or pipe the eggnog filling on half the cookies and sandwich them with the other half.

# Spooky Gingerbread Trees

1 x batch Basic Gingerbread
   Dough (page 46)
1cm (½in) edible pearls or white
   chocolate balls
black edible ink pen
black lustre dust
1 x batch Royal Icing (page
   47) (or you could use vanilla
   buttercream – see page 22)
green gel food colour
brown gel food colour
sprinkles

I made these a couple of years ago and they went down a treat with
friends and family. The basics are the same as with any other gingerbread
cookie – gingerbread and icing – but with just a couple of additions you
can produce an original and fun variation. If you don't have a tree-shaped
cookie cutter, simply draw the shape on card or baking paper, cut out
and use as a template.

Make the gingerbread dough according to the instructions on page 46.

Cut out 14–16 tree shapes using a template or cookie cutter and place
on a baking tray lined with baking paper.

Bake according to the instructions on page 46, then let them cool
completely on a wire rack before decorating.

For Tim-Burton-style eyes, take the edible pearls or white chocolate balls
and use the edible ink pen to draw little black dots on them for pupils,
then brush some black lustre dust around the outsides. Set aside.

Colour some of your royal icing (or buttercream) with brown food colour
for the tree trunks and some with green for the foliage. Pop into separate
piping bags fitted with small star nozzles.

First, attach the eyes to the trees with a little icing so they stick. Next,
pipe the brown trunks. Using the green icing, pipe some eyelids above
and below the eyeballs, then pipe a succession of green shell shapes to
create the foliage, starting from the base of the tree and working your
way upwards. Finish with sprinkles to make them look like decorated
Christmas trees.

MAKES 12

# Chocolate Orange Gingerbread Cauldrons

## FOR THE CHOCOLATE ORANGE GINGERBREAD

400g (14oz/3 cups) plain (all-purpose) flour, plus extra for dusting

60g (2¼oz/6 Tbsp) cocoa powder

½ tsp baking powder

2 Tbsp ground ginger

1 tsp ground cinnamon

1 tsp ground cardamom

½ tsp ground nutmeg

150g (⅔ cup) unsalted butter

100g (3½oz/½ cup) dark brown sugar

125ml (4fl oz/½ cup) black treacle or molasses

1 tsp bicarbonate of soda (baking soda)

zest of 2 oranges

1 tsp vanilla bean paste

1 egg

## FOR THE ORANGE BUTTERCREAM

115g (½ cup) unsalted butter, at room temperature

400g (14oz/3 cups) icing (confectioners') sugar, or as needed, sifted

1 Tbsp finely grated orange zest

5 Tbsp orange juice, or as needed

green gel food colour

yellow gel food colour

red gel food colour

## TO FINISH

mixed Christmas/Halloween sprinkles

If you happen to have my two previous books, you will know that it has become a tradition of sorts to have one of the recipes come from the mind of Michael Chakraverty, who stressed alongside me during our year in the *Bake Off* tent. This time he has given me a recipe for chocolate orange gingerbread (he just loves chocolate orange) and I've decided to turn this fragrant dough into Christmas cauldrons filled with goodies.

❧

For the chocolate orange gingerbread, sift together the flour, cocoa, baking powder and spices. Set aside.

In a saucepan set over a medium-low heat, melt together the butter, dark brown sugar and treacle, then stir through the bicarbonate of soda. Add the orange zest and vanilla bean paste to the mixture and allow to cool a little before stirring through the dry ingredients, followed by the egg.

Bring the mixture together into a dough, then divide it in half, flatten into discs and wrap in clingfilm (plastic wrap). Chill overnight.

The next day, roll out one half of the dough on a lightly floured surface to 5mm (¼in) thick. Cut into 12 cauldrons using a 6-cm (2½-in) diameter cauldron cookie cutter and place on a baking tray lined with baking paper, spaced 2.5cm (1in) apart to allow room to spread during baking. Chill before baking to help them keep their shape.

Meanwhile, preheat the oven to 180°C (160°C fan/350°F/Gas mark 4).

Bake for 7–8 minutes until lightly brown, then allow them to cool on a wire rack.

To make the semi-circles filled with sprinkles, roll out the other half of the dough and cut into 12 circles with a 6-cm (2½-in) round cookie cutter. To mould to the right shape, use a silicon semi-circle or half-

PLEASE TURN OVER

sphere baking tray for baking 4cm (1½ in) domes and turn it upside-down on a baking tray. Arrange the semi-circles over the dome shapes and bake as before.

For the buttercream, beat the butter in a stand mixer until light and fluffy. Add the icing sugar and continue beating on a low speed until fully incorporated, then add the orange zest and juice and mix. If the consistency is too runny, add more icing sugar; if it is too dry, add more orange juice.

Separate the buttercream into three bowls and colour one with green food colour, one with yellow and one with red. Fill three piping bags with each colour and cut off the ends.

Fill the semi-circles with sprinkles and use a little buttercream to glue the cauldrons to them.

Pipe green buttercream on the tops as bubbling goo coming out of the cauldron and top it with some more of the sprinkles. To make the flames, pipe them on with the yellow buttercream and add some red details on top. It helps to shape them with a toothpick.

# Russian Mushroom Cookies

575g (1lb 4½oz/4¼ cups) plain
   (all-purpose) flour
2 tsp ground ginger
1 tsp ground cinnamon
½ tsp bicarbonate of soda
   (baking soda)
pinch of salt
175g (¾ cup) unsalted butter,
   at room temperature
200g (7oz/1 cup) caster
   (superfine) sugar
160g (5¾oz/⅔ cup) mayonnaise
2 large eggs

**TO DECORATE**
1 x batch Royal Icing (page 47)
150g (5oz/1 cup) poppy seeds
225g (8oz) dark chocolate,
   chopped, plus a little extra,
   melted, to use as glue if
   shaping the cookies by hand
240ml (8fl oz/1 cup) double
   (heavy) cream

These traditional Russian cookies make the perfect holiday treat –
either to eat or to gift to friends and family. I am giving these mushroom
cookies, or *gribochky*, a delicate touch of ginger because it just works
beautifully. Since I love old kitchenalia, I happen to have an old
Lithuanian mushroom cookie pan (it bakes about 10 at a time and goes
on the hob (stove) – it can be sourced online), but you don't need one
to make these tiny cookies – they can be shaped by hand.

ﮩﮩﮩ

Sift together the flour, ginger, cinnamon, bicarbonate of soda and salt
in a medium bowl and set aside.

In a stand mixer fitted with the paddle attachment, beat the butter and
sugar on medium speed until light and fluffy. Add the mayonnaise and
continue mixing, making sure to scrape down the sides and bottom of the
bowl from time to time. Add the eggs, one at a time, and continue mixing
until fully incorporated. Slowly mix in the dry ingredients on a low speed.
The batter will be soft but pliable.

Tip the dough onto the work surface and bring it together into a ball.
Cover with clingfilm (plastic wrap) and chill in the refrigerator for
15 minutes.

If you can get hold of a mushroom cookie pan, roughly form pieces of the
dough into mushroom shapes and place in the pan. Cook over a medium
heat for 3 minutes, then flip it over and cook for another minute or so.
Release and repeat process with the rest of the dough.

If you haven't got a mushroom pan, preheat the oven to 200°C (180°C
fan/400°F/Gas mark 6) and line two baking trays with baking paper.

Divide the dough in half. Shape one half of the dough into mushroom
caps – about 2.5cm (1in) in diameter – by making a flattened ball and

PLEASE
TURN OVER

63

These mushrooms bear a resemblance to *Boletus edulis* (ceps or porcini), which often grows alongside *Amanita muscaria*, the fairy-tale mushroom with a red cap and white warts that we see in so many Christmas scenes. To decorate your mushrooms like these, colour some white chocolate with powder-based red food colour for the caps and use some white royal icing to pipe the warts. Instead of the poppy seeds, you can rub some moss green gel food colour with your fingertips into shredded coconut and dip the base of the stems in it.

using your thumb to hollow out the middle. Shape the other half of the dough into stem shapes, about 2.5cm (1in) long. Place on the baking trays (you will need to work in batches) and bake for 10–12 minutes, rotating the pans halfway through. Cool on a wire rack and repeat the process until all the dough is used up.

Meanwhile, put the royal icing into a medium bowl and thin it out slightly with a little water to get a dipping consistency. Cover and set aside.

When cool, you can decorate your mushrooms. If they were baked in a cookie pan, they will be ready to decorate. Dip the stem ends in the royal icing and shake the excess off. Let dry for 15 minutes or so (egg cartons are very useful for this). The bottoms will still be a little wet, so dip them into the poppy seeds at this point, rolling the base around a little, then leave to dry completely.

If you are shaping the cookies by hand, first stick the caps to the stems using a little melted chocolate. Once cooled, follow the previous step.

While the cookies are drying, make the chocolate ganache by placing the chopped chocolate in a medium bowl. Heat the cream in a small saucepan over a medium heat until just about to simmer, then pour it over the chocolate, let it stand for 2–3 minutes, then stir with a silicon spatula until the chocolate is fully melted.

Dip the mushroom caps into the chocolate ganache and leave to dry in the egg carton between the triangles so that the cap hardly touches the surface.

# Ginger & Lemon Candy Cane Snakes

230g (1 cup) unsalted butter,
   at room temperature
200g (7oz/1 cup) caster
   (superfine) sugar
1 Tbsp finely grated lemon zest
2 Tbsp lemon juice
1½ tsp ground ginger
½ tsp ground cinnamon
½ tsp baking powder
½ tsp salt
1 large egg
385g (13½oz/scant 3 cups)
   plain (all-purpose) flour
red gel food colour
red round sprinkles or candies
   for the eyes
50g (1¾oz) Royal Icing
   (page 46)

**Lemon shortbread is one of my favourite biscuits and ginger marries well with lemon. Candy canes are a classic for Christmas. Snakes are spooky. Mash all three things together and we get candy cane snake cookies with a lovely lemony touch.**

ellee

In a stand mixer fitted with the paddle attachment, mix the butter and sugar on medium speed until light and fluffy. Add the lemon zest and juice, ginger, cinnamon, baking powder, salt and egg and continue mixing. Add the flour and mix on a low speed until fully combined, scraping down the sides and bottom of the bowl from time to time.

Remove half the dough from the bowl and colour the remaining dough with the red food colour. Cover both doughs with clingfilm (plastic wrap) and refrigerate for 3–4 hours, or overnight.

Preheat the oven to 195°C (175°C fan/375°F/Gas mark 5). Line two baking trays with baking paper or silicon mats.

Shape the white dough into a 20cm (8in) log. Divide the red dough in half and form two log shapes the same length as the white one. Form into a single log with a stripe of red on each side of the white. On the countertop, use your hands to roll out the log (without twisting at this stage) to the desired thickness you want them to be. Next, roll each end of the log in opposite directions with your fingertips, working along its length, to create the red and white twist effect. Cut into pieces, 18cm (7in) long. Shape one end of each into a point for the tail and shape the head at the other end. Roll them inwards. If you find it difficult to shape the dough without breaking it into one long log shape, mould the snakes individually into 18cm–20cm (7–8in) logs. Place the cookies on your prepared trays and bake for 8–10 minutes, or until the edges begin to brown. Cool completely on a wire rack.

Once the cookies are fully cooled, use a little royal icing to attach red sprinkles at each side of the head for the eyes.

# Phases of the Moon Polvorones

400g (14oz/3 cups) plain (all-purpose) flour, plus extra for dusting

125g (4½oz/1¼ cups) ground almonds

200g (7oz/14 Tbsp) lard

150g (5oz/1 cup) icing (confectioners') sugar, plus extra for dusting

2 tsp ground ginger

1 tsp ground cinnamon

*Polvorones* are to Spanish Christmas what mince pies are to the British. There's no Christmas without polvorones or *turrón* (nougat) in Spain. *Polvo* means 'dust', and it refers to the way this cookie turns to dust when you bite into it because it contains lard rather than butter. This ancient recipe only requires four ingredients, although I have added some ginger (of course) and cinnamon to them. As the polvorones are traditionally dusted with icing (confectioners') sugar on top, they make the perfect candidates for representing the phases of the moon.

*ellee*

Preheat the oven to 200°C (180°C fan/400°F/Gas mark 6).

Mix the flour and ground almonds on a large baking tray. Toast in the oven for about 40 minutes, stirring every 10 minutes or so to help it toast evenly. Once it's golden, remove from the oven and let cool completely.

In a stand mixer fitted with the paddle attachment, beat the lard and sugar until light and fluffy. Add the toasted flour mixture, ginger and cinnamon, and mix to combine. Bring together into a dough, then cover with clingfilm (plastic wrap) and refrigerate for 15 minutes.

Line two baking trays with baking paper or a silicon mat.

Roll out the dough on a lightly floured surface to 1cm (½in) thick and cut out 12 discs with a 5cm (2in) cookie cutter. Re-roll the trimmings and cut the rest. Place them on your prepared trays and bake for 15 minutes. Leave to cool on the tray as they are extremely delicate.

Once cooled, use a piece of paper to cover part of the cookies as shown before dusting with icing sugar to create the different phases of the moon: new moon, waxing crescent, waxing half, waxing gibbous, full moon, waning gibbous, waning half and waning crescent.

## NOTE

If you would like to make a sun polvorón for the moon ones to be displayed with, bake in a sun silicon mould. Once cooled, brush with a little sugar syrup and stick gold leaf on top.

# White Chocolate Gingerbread Cookies

150g (⅔ cup) unsalted butter,
   at room temperature
200g (7oz/1 cup) dark brown
   sugar
2 large eggs
1 tsp vanilla extract
300g (10½oz/2¼ cups) plain
   (all-purpose) flour
1 tsp ground ginger
¾ tsp ground cinnamon
½ tsp freshly grated nutmeg
¼ tsp ground cloves (optional)
1½ tsp baking powder
½ tsp bicarbonate of soda
   (baking soda)
½ tsp salt
300g (10½oz) good-quality
   white chocolate, chopped
   into chunks

I love a gooey chocolate chip cookie, and during the winter months adding a gentle touch of gingerbread spices makes these cookies the perfect thing to bake. The perfect snack, in fact, to sit with in front of a fire with a good book and a gingerbread latte (see page 100).

In a stand mixer fitted with the paddle attachment, beat the butter and sugar on medium-high speed until light and fluffy. Add the eggs and the vanilla and continue mixing. Reduce the speed to medium-low and add the flour, ginger, cinnamon, nutmeg, cloves (if using), baking powder, bicarbonate of soda and salt. Continue mixing until all the ingredients are well combined. Add the chocolate chunks. Wrap the dough in clingfilm (plastic wrap) and refrigerate for 45 minutes.

Preheat the oven to 200°C (180°C fan/400°F/Gas mark 6) and line a large baking tray with baking paper or a silicon mat.

Using an ice-cream scoop, scoop 10–12 dollops of dough onto the baking tray, spaced 5cm (2in) apart, as the cookies will spread as they cook. Bake for 12–14 minutes.

Allow them to cool on the baking tray, if you can resist eating them straight away.

# Gingerbread Viennese Wreaths

**FOR THE BISCUITS**
200g (7oz/1½ cups) plain (all-purpose) flour
2 tsp ground ginger
1 tsp cornflour (cornstarch)
½ tsp baking powder
200g (¾ cup plus 2 Tbsp) unsalted butter, at room temperature
2½ Tbsp icing (confectioners') sugar
1 tsp vanilla extract
green food colour

**FOR THE GANACHE**
100g (3½oz) white chocolate, finely chopped
300ml (10½oz/1¼ cups) double (heavy) or whipping cream

**TO DECORATE**
red sprinkles
icing (confectioners') sugar

This classic buttery biscuit gets a hint of spice and everything nice for the holidays. I've chosen to fill them with white chocolate ganache, but any other buttercream recipe listed in this book would work, as they are all complementary to ginger.

*elle*

Preheat the oven to 200°C (180°C fan/400°F/Gas mark 6) and line two baking trays with baking paper.

Sift together the flour, ginger, cornflour and baking powder, and set aside.

In a stand mixer fitted with the paddle attachment, beat the butter and icing sugar on medium-high speed until light and fluffy. Add the vanilla and keep mixing. Slowly add the dry ingredients, then add the food colour, a tiny bit at a time, until you get the desired tone.

Put the batter into a piping bag fitted with a large star nozzle and pipe 20 round circles on the baking trays, about 7cm (2¾in) in diameter, leaving a space of 4cm (1½in) between them.

Bake for 10–12 minutes, turning and swapping the trays halfway through. Cool on a wire rack.

To make the ganache, put the chopped chocolate in a medium bowl. Heat the cream in a small saucepan over a medium heat until just about to simmer, remove from the heat and pour over the white chocolate. Let it stand for a couple of minutes, then gently mix with a silicon spatula. Leave to firm up to a spreadable consistency, then transfer to a piping bag fitted with a star nozzle.

Pipe the ganache on half of the biscuits and top with the other halves. Stick some red sprinkles on top with a little of the white chocolate ganache and sprinkle with icing sugar.

# Krampus & The Grinch Ginger Cookies

200g (7oz/1½ cups) plain (all-purpose) flour
½ tsp baking powder
1 tsp ground ginger
¼ tsp ground cinnamon
pinch of salt
1 large egg
1 Tbsp vanilla extract
55ml (1¾fl oz/3 Tbsp plus 2 tsp) vegetable oil
150g (5oz/¾ cup) caster (superfine) sugar
red gel food colour
green gel food colour
100g (3½oz/¾ cup) icing (confectioners') sugar, sifted

**TO DECORATE**
100g (3½oz) yellow fondant
100g (3½oz) red fondant
black edible paint or pen
50g (1¾oz) Royal Icing (page 47)

**Give these festive cookies a touch of evil by simply adding a suggestive eye from two of the most notorious Christmas villains. These crackled cookies have more of a cake texture and a hint of ginger flavour. Be sure to use gel food colour to get a vibrant shade and to mix by hand rather than using an electric mixer.**

Sift the flour, baking powder, ginger, cinnamon and salt into a medium bowl and set aside.

In a large mixing bowl whisk together the egg, vanilla, vegetable oil and sugar until fully combined. Add the dry ingredients and mix to a dough.

Divide the dough in half and add red food colour to one half and green to the other. Cover both with clingfilm (plastic wrap) and refrigerate for 30 minutes.

Preheat the oven to 200°C (180°C fan/400°F/Gas mark 6). Line a baking tray with baking paper or a silicon mat.

Take a tablespoon of dough, shape into a ball and roll in the icing sugar. Repeat until you have used up all the dough. Place on the baking tray, spaced 5cm (2in) apart, and bake for 12–14 minutes.

As soon as you remove the cookies from the oven, make an indentation in the middle of each one where the eye will be placed. A ball modelling tool is helpful for this. Leave the cookies to cool on a wire rack.

While the cookies are cooling make your Grinch and Krampus eyes. Roll 10 balls of yellow fondant and 10 of red. Let them harden a bit, then paint or draw a black line on the red balls for the Krampus eyes and a black dot or horseshoe shape on the yellow balls for the Grinch ones.

Attach the eyes to the middle of the cookies (yellow eyes on the green cookies and red eyes on the red cookies) with a little royal icing.

# Desserts

# Pumpkin & Ginger Cream Cheesecake

## FOR THE CREAM TOPPING
240ml (8fl oz/1 cup) double (heavy) cream
240ml (8fl oz/1 cup) sour cream
3 Tbsp dark rum
½ tsp vanilla extract
60g (2oz/¼ cup) crystallized ginger, finely chopped

## FOR THE BASE
75g (2½oz/¾ cup) digestive biscuit or graham cracker crumbs
50g (1¾oz/½ cup) pecans, finely chopped
50g (1¾oz/¼ packed cup) brown sugar
4 Tbsp salted butter, melted

## FOR THE FILLING
1 x 425g (15oz) can of pumpkin purée
3 large eggs
100g (3½oz/½ packed cup) brown sugar
1 tsp vanilla extract
1½ tsp ground cinnamon
½ tsp ground ginger
½ tsp ground nutmeg
¼ tsp salt
680g (1lb 8oz) full-fat cream cheese
100g (3½oz/½ cup) caster (superfine) sugar
1 Tbsp plain (all-purpose) flour

## TO DECORATE (OPTIONAL)
candied oranges

This isn't your standard cheesecake; this is a cheesecake worthy of the place of honour at your holiday table. This recipe was given to me when I was just a teenager at high school in Las Vegas. I did however reduce the amount of sugar in it, because it was just a touch too sweet, but of course you can adapt to your liking.

◦◦◦◦

Make the cream topping first, as it ideally needs to be refrigerated overnight. Whip the cream and sour cream in a stand mixer fitted with the whisk attachment until stiff peaks form. Fold in the rum, vanilla and ginger. Cover and refrigerate for 6–8 hours, or overnight.

For the base, place the biscuit crumbs, pecans and sugar in a medium bowl and whisk together. Stir in the melted butter and press the mixture into the base and halfway up the sides of a 23cm (9in) springform cake tin. Refrigerate for 1 hour.

Preheat the oven to 200°C (180°C fan/400°F/Gas mark 6).

For the filling, mix the pumpkin purée, eggs, brown sugar, vanilla, spices, and salt in a medium bowl. Set aside.

In a stand mixer fitted with the paddle attachment, beat the cream cheese and caster sugar until well combined, then add the flour and pumpkin mixture, and continue mixing until smooth.

Pour the filling into the base and bake for 50–55 minutes until set. Leave to cool completely.

Spread the cream topping over the cheesecake and refrigerate for a further 6–8 hours until set.

If you choose to decorate it, place some rosemary sprigs all around the edge and top with candied orange slices.

# Pear & Gingerbread Crumble

200g (7oz/1½ cups) plain (all-purpose) flour
60g (2oz/5 Tbsp) light muscovado sugar
1 tsp ground ginger
½ tsp ground cinnamon
100g (7 Tbsp) unsalted butter, cold and cubed, plus 1 Tbsp for the filling
40g (1½oz/½ cup) pecans, roughly chopped
900g (2lb) pears (about 5–6), peeled, cored and chopped into 2–3cm (¾–1¼in) chunks
2 tsp demerara (light brown) sugar
100g (3½oz) stem ginger in syrup, chopped, plus 1 Tbsp syrup from the jar
1 cinnamon stick
2 whole cloves

**TO SERVE**
custard, cream or vanilla ice cream

**The only dessert I regularly made while at university in the UK was crumble. It was my first experience of a warm dessert, as that is just unheard of in Spain – even the rice pudding is served cold on my home turf. This particular crumble tastes like the essence of autumn/winter – warming and satisfying.**

☙

Preheat the oven to 200°C (180°C fan/400°F/Gas mark 6).

Combine the flour, light muscovado sugar, ground ginger, cinnamon and 100g of butter in a large bowl and rub together with your fingers until it resembles breadcrumbs. Mix in the pecans and set aside.

In a large saucepan (or a cast-iron pan) set over a medium heat, melt the extra tablespoon of butter, add the chopped pears, demerara sugar, stem ginger and syrup, cinnamon stick and cloves, and cook for 4–5 minutes.

Remove the cloves and cinnamon stick and transfer the mixture to a baking dish (or, if you used a cast-iron pan to cook the pears in, leave them in the pan). Top the cooked pears with the crumble mixture and bake for 30 minutes or until the liquid is bubbling up and the edges are golden.

Serve warm with custard, cream or vanilla ice cream.

# Gingerbread Pumpkin Pie-thon

**FOR THE GINGERBREAD PASTRY**

400g (14oz/3 cups) plain (all-purpose) flour, plus extra for dusting

80g (3oz) icing (confectioners') sugar

2½ tsp ground ginger

1 tsp ground cinnamon

½ tsp freshly grated nutmeg

¼ tsp ground cloves

¼ tsp salt

250g (1 cup plus 2 Tbsp) unsalted butter, cold and cubed

3 egg yolks, plus 1, beaten, for egg wash

50ml (1¾fl oz/3 Tbsp plus 1 tsp) ice-cold water

**FOR THE FILLING**

1 x 425g (15oz) can pumpkin purée

1 large egg plus 1 egg yolk

235ml (8fl oz/1 cup) evaporated milk

200g (7oz/1 cup) caster (superfine) sugar

1 tsp salt

1 tsp ground cinnamon

¼ tsp ground ginger

¼ tsp ground cloves

¼ tsp salt

1 Tbsp plain (all-purpose) flour

**TO SERVE**

200ml (7fl oz/scant 1 cup) double (heavy) or cream

2 Tbsp Ginger Syrup (page 123 or from a jar of stem ginger)

There's no way I would write a cookbook without including some spooky twists along the way. Pumpkin pie remains one of my favourite sweet bakes, so this autumn–winter classic deserved a look-in. This time, I've given this all-American dessert a gingerbread pastry base.

ellee

For the gingerbread pastry, combine the flour, icing sugar, spices and salt in a bowl (it can be done in the food processor, too). Add the cubed butter and rub it into the flour until the mixture resembles breadcrumbs. Add the 3 egg yolks and water and continue to bring the dough together. Tip onto a clean work surface and knead a couple of times, then wrap the dough in clingfilm (plastic wrap) and refrigerate for 30–45 minutes.

Remove the dough from the refrigerator and roll to 5mm (¼in) thick on a lightly floured surface. Line a 23cm (9in) pie dish with the pastry and trim the edges. Use the leftover pastry to make a long roll and shape into a snake by pinching the neck and shaping the head, and making the tail thinner than the body. Imitate snake markings in the surface of the back with a sharp knife, or alternatively press on the back of a silicon mat or mould. Cut out some leaf shapes with cookie cutters. Place on a baking tray lined with baking paper, cover with clingfilm and refrigerate all the pastry elements until ready to bake.

Preheat the oven to 190°C (170°C fan/375°F/Gas mark 5).

Combine all the filling ingredients in a medium bowl – the mixture will be quite liquid, but it will set in the oven. Pour the pie filling into the pastry case. Brush the pastry edges and decorations on the baking tray with egg wash. Bake the pie for 30–40 minutes, or until the pie filling sets. Bake the decorations for 12 minutes.

Leave the pie to cool, then place the decorations on top. Before serving, whip the cream with the ginger syrup until soft peaks form. Serve each slice of pie with a dollop of ginger cream on top.

# Gingerbread Gelato

450ml (16fl oz/scant 2 cups) double (heavy) cream
480ml (16½fl oz/2 cups) whole milk
165g (6oz/generous ¾ cup) dark brown sugar
80g (2¾oz/¼ cup) black treacle or molasses
115g (4oz/1 cup) fresh root ginger, peeled and cut into 2cm (¾in) pieces
7 egg yolks
1 Tbsp vanilla extract
1 tsp ground cinnamon
½ tsp freshly grated nutmeg
¼ tsp ground cloves
pinch of salt
1–2 gingerbread biscuits, crushed
115g (4oz/1 cup) stem ginger, chopped (optional)
gingerbread biscuits of your choice, to decorate

**Gingerbread makes for a fantastic ice cream flavour. Here, I have served it quite simply in vintage Babycham glasses, decorated with little gingerbread fawns, but I have also successfully used this gelato to make a bombe Alaska, covered in torched meringue, for another showstopping Christmas dessert.**

In a large saucepan over a medium heat, whisk together the cream, milk, sugar, treacle and chopped fresh ginger until the sugar is dissolved. Bring to a simmer, then remove from the heat before it comes to the boil. Leave to cool for 30–40 minutes.

Pour the infused cream mixture through a sieve to remove the ginger and set aside.

In a large saucepan over a low heat, combine the egg yolks, vanilla, spices and salt, then slowly add the cream mixture while whisking constantly. Keep whisking until it forms a custard that covers the back of a wooden spoon.

Transfer to a bowl and cover the surface of the custard with clingfilm (plastic wrap) to avoid a skin forming. Refrigerate overnight.

The next day, pour the custard into an ice-cream maker and churn according to the manufacturer's instructions. Add the crushed gingerbread and stem ginger, if using, 2–3 minutes before the machine stops churning.

Decorate with gingerbread biscuits of your choice.

# Gingerbread Candelabra Dome Cake

**FOR THE CAKE**

non-stick baking spray or
  vegetable oil
375g (13oz/scant 3 cups) plain
  (all-purpose) flour
1 tsp baking powder
1 tsp bicarbonate of soda
  (baking soda)
4 Tbsp ground ginger
1 Tbsp ground cinnamon
½ tsp freshly grated nutmeg
½ tsp salt
250g (1 cup plus 2 Tbsp)
  unsalted butter
250g (9oz/1¼ cups) demerara
  (light brown) sugar
120g (4¼oz/generous ⅓ cup)
  black treacle or molasses
300ml (10½fl oz/1¼ cups)
  whole milk
3 large eggs

**FOR THE CHOCOLATE SCROLL
DECORATIONS**

300g (10½oz) dark chocolate,
  chopped
gold edible spray paint
12 gold birthday candles
gold edible paint

**FOR THE GINGER MERINGUE**

4 large egg whites, at room
  temperature
200g (7oz/1 cup) granulated
  sugar
2½ Tbsp Ginger Syrup
  (page 123 or from a jar of
  stem ginger)

I'm not a fan of Christmas pudding, however I love the drama of setting it on fire on the way to the table, so I've created an even more dramatic dessert that is truly a Christmas showstopper. This dessert is inspired by pastry chef Sedar Yener's Bombe Alaska. The cake itself is super easy, it's the decoration that requires a bit more patience, but the result is so worth it. After all, if you can't make a bit more of an effort at this time of the year, when can you?

You will need the printed templates on page 145 and four large acetate sheets to make the chocolate scroll decorations.

ℓℓℓℓ

Preheat the oven to 200°C (180°C fan/400°F/Gas mark 6). Line a 24-cm (9½in) metal mixing bowl with non-stick foil. It will crunch a bit, but this is okay. Spray the foil with non-stick baking spray. Set aside.

Sift the flour, baking powder, bicarbonate of soda, spices and salt into a bowl and set aside.

Melt the butter, sugar and treacle in a large saucepan over a low-medium heat, stirring constantly until well combined. Slowly add the milk and warm through. Remove from the heat and mix in the dry ingredients until fully combined, then add the eggs, one by one, beating after each addition.

Pour the batter into your prepared bowl and bake for 35–40 minutes, or until a skewer inserted in the middle comes out clean.

For the chocolate scroll decorations, place your printed template on a countertop with an acetate sheet on top. Melt your chocolate at 30-second intervals in the microwave, then pour into a piping bag. Cut the tip from the end and pipe the scroll shape. Repeat on each sheet of acetate so you have four scrolls. Let them set fully.

PLEASE
TURN OVER

Transfer the remaining melted chocolate to another piping bag and cut the tip slightly smaller this time. Pipe again on top of the chocolate scrolls to decorate and give them depth. Leave to set again.

When dry, turn the chocolate scrolls over on their acetate sheets and pipe the backs in exactly the same way as just described. Leave to set.

Paint all the scrolls with edible gold spray paint on both sides.

To make the ginger meringue, whisk the egg whites and sugar by hand in a medium heat-resistant bowl until combined. Place the bowl over a pan of simmering water, making sure the bottom of the bowl doesn't touch the water. Whisk the mixture constantly until the sugar is fully dissolved and you can no longer feel any granules between your fingers, or until the mixture reaches 50–60°C (120–140°F) on a sugar thermometer. Remove the bowl from the heat and beat with a hand-held electric mixer until you achieve stiff peaks and the sides of the bowl are no longer warm to the touch. Mix in the ginger syrup.

To assemble, use a palette knife to cover the dome cake with most of the ginger meringue and smooth it out as much as you can. Mark a cross with a knife or skewer in the dome, dividing it into four sections. Put the rest of the meringue into a piping bag, cut the end off and pipe some decorative shells or scrolls around the base of the dome and in each of the four sections. Lightly toast the surface of the meringue with a kitchen blowtorch.

Place the chocolate scrolls onto the dome in the four sections marked. Dip the bases of the candles into some melted chocolate and attach them to the scrolls in equally spaced intervals – three on each scroll – holding them in place until the melted chocolate sets. Paint the hardened chocolate with a little gold edible paint.

Pat yourself on the back and wait for the compliments when you serve this masterpiece at the table.

# Gingerbread, Chocolate & Cranberry Trifle

## FOR THE CRANBERRY CURD
225g (8oz) fresh cranberries
120ml (½ cup) orange juice
2 tbsp orange zest
200g (7oz/1 cup) granulated sugar
3 eggs yolks and 1 whole egg
4 tbsp unsalted butter, cubed

## FOR THE SPONGE
140g (5oz/1 cup) plain (all-purpose) flour
1½ tbsp cocoa powder
¼ tsp bicarbonate of soda (baking soda)
¼ tsp salt
1 tsp ground ginger
1 tsp ground cinnamon
½ tsp ground nutmeg
¼ tsp ground cloves
115g (½ cup) unsalted butter, at room temperature
110g (3½oz/ ½ cup) dark brown sugar
2 eggs
½ tbsp vanilla extract
3 tbsp buttermilk
140g (5oz/scant ½ cup) golden syrup

## FOR THE MASCARPONE CREAM
360g (12¾oz/generous 1½ cups) mascarpone cheese
480ml (16½fl oz/scant 2 cups) whipping cream
100g (3½oz/generous ¾ cup) icing (confectioners') sugar
1 tbsp vanilla extract
2 tbsp orange zest
2 tbsp orange liqueur (optional)

sparklers, to decorate

Trifle is such a classic British dessert, however I must say this Christmas version is a wonderful adaptation to try. Cranberry curd substitutes the jam, mascarpone cream will always elevate the flavour of any whipped cream and the sponge is a chocolate gingerbread delight.

≈≈≈

For the cranberry curd, combine the cranberries and orange juice in a small saucepan over a medium heat. Cook until the cranberries start to pop and the orange juice starts boiling. Push the mixture through a sieve, pressing it well with a wooden spoon and making sure to scrape the purée from underneath. Put the purée back into the pan and set aside.

Preheat the oven to 180°C (160°C fan/350°F/Gas mark 4) and grease a 46 x 33cm (18 x 13in) baking tray that is about 5cm (2in) deep.

For the sponge, mix the flour, cocoa powder, bicarbonate of soda, salt and spices in a medium bowl and set aside.

In a stand mixer fitted with the paddle attachment, or with a hand-held mixer, beat the butter and brown sugar for 2 minutes on medium-high speed. Add the eggs, one at a time, then the vanilla, and finally the buttermilk and golden syrup. Turn the speed down and add the dry ingredients, and mix until fully incorporated. Pour into your prepared tray and bake for 30 minutes, or until a toothpick inserted in the middle comes out clean. Allow to cool, then cut the sponge into 4cm (1½in) squares.

For the mascarpone cream, whip the mascarpone cheese for 1 minute in a small bowl. Add the cream and beat with a whisk until fully whipped, then add the icing sugar and continue mixing until fully incorporated. Finally, mix in the vanilla, orange zest and liqueur.

To assemble, layer half the sponge squares tightly in the base of a 23cm (9in) trifle bowl. Layer half the cranberry curd on top and spread it evenly, then spread over half the mascarpone cream. Repeat the layers, ending with cream, and decorate with some sparklers.

# A Partridge in a Pear Tart

**FOR THE GINGERBREAD PASTRY**

400g (14oz/3 cups) plain (all-purpose) flour, plus extra for dusting

80g (2¾oz/9 Tbsp) icing (confectioners') sugar

2½ tsp ground ginger

1 tsp ground cinnamon

½ tsp freshly grated nutmeg

¼ tsp ground cloves

¼ tsp salt

250g (1 cup plus 2 Tbsp) unsalted butter, cold and cubed

3 egg yolks, plus 1, beaten, for egg wash

50ml (1¾fl oz/3 Tbsp plus 1 tsp) ice-cold water

**FOR THE FILLING**

125g (9 Tbsp) unsalted butter, at room temperature

125g (4½oz/scant ⅔ cup) demerara (light brown) or golden caster (superfine) sugar

2 large eggs

125g (4½oz/1 cup plus 1 Tbsp) ground almonds

2 Tbsp plain (all-purpose) flour

2 balls of stem ginger, finely chopped

3 Tbsp stem ginger syrup (from the jar)

1 tsp vanilla extract

3 ripe pears, peeled, halved and cored

handful of flaked (slivered) almonds

Since I planted a pear tree in my garden, I can't help but develop pear-based desserts. This one is a favourite of mine. I've always loved the combination of pear and almond, and adding a warming touch of stem ginger elevates this tart to another level. You can use store-bought pastry for this recipe, but I like to add an extra touch of ginger and make it from scratch. To decorate the tart, I thought a nod to the partridge in the pear tree that marks the first day of Christmas seemed rather appropriate.

For the gingerbread pastry, combine the flour, icing sugar, spices and salt in a bowl (it can be done in a food processor, too). Add the cubed butter and rub it in until the mixture resembles breadcrumbs. Add the egg yolks and water, and continue to bring the dough together. Tip it out onto a clean work surface and knead a couple of times, then wrap the dough clingfilm (plastic wrap) and refrigerate for 30 minutes.

Preheat the oven to 200°C (180°C fan/400°F/Gas mark 6).

Remove the dough from the refrigerator and roll to 5mm (¼in) thick on a lightly floured surface. Line a 23cm (9in) pie dish or fluted tart tin with the pastry and trim the edges (keep the offcuts). Prick the base of the tart with a fork and line with baking paper weighted down with baking beans or rice. Blind-bake the pastry case for 15 minutes, then remove the beans and paper and bake for a further 10 minutes, or until golden. Leave to cool.

For the filling, in a stand mixer fitted with the paddle attachment, mix the butter and sugar on medium speed until light and fluffy. Add the eggs, one at a time, then mix in the ground almonds, flour, chopped stem ginger, syrup and vanilla.

Spread the filling mixture evenly over the pastry base and place the pear halves on top, forming a circle. To create the pastry pear tree, use the pastry offcuts: roll into long logs that you can arrange around the pear

halves, twisting and turning to create a tree shape. Cut out some little leaves with a pastry or cookie cutter and make a little partridge to sit in one of the branches. Attach these with a little water. Refrigerate the tart for 20 minutes.

Brush the pastry with egg wash and bake for 30–35 minutes, or until golden brown, adding the flaked almonds halfway through in between the tree branches. If you feel the top of the tart is browning too quickly, cover it with foil.

# Sticky Toffee Gingerbread Pudding

non-stick baking spray or
  vegetable oil
225g (8oz) whole Medjool
  dates, pitted and chopped
180ml (6fl oz/¾ cup) boiling
  water
1 tsp vanilla extract
175g (6oz/1⅓ cups) plain (all-
  purpose) flour
1¾ tsp baking powder
1 tsp bicarbonate of soda
  (baking soda)
1 tsp ground cinnamon
¾ tsp ground ginger
pinch of ground cloves
85g (6 Tbsp) unsalted butter,
  softened
140g (5oz/scant ¾ cup)
  demerara (light brown) sugar
2 eggs
2 Tbsp black treacle
100ml (3½fl oz/scant ½ cup)
  milk

**FOR THE SAUCE**
50g (3½ Tbsp) unsalted butter,
  cubed
180g (6¼oz/scant 1 cup) light
  muscovado sugar
1 Tbsp black treacle
pinch of salt
225ml (7¾ fl oz/1 cup) double
  (heavy) cream

**TO SERVE**
vanilla ice cream, cream or
  custard

Sticky toffee pudding is by far my favourite British bake. It's incredibly moist and gooey, with a real depth of flavour. Adding a touch of ginger just gives this classic dessert a wonderful twist, perfect for the colder months since it's served warm. Instead of a baking tin, you could also use a bundt tin or even an old ceramic jelly mould to bake this pudding in.

ﾟﾟ

Preheat the oven to 200°C (180°C fan/400°F/Gas mark 6). Spray a 20-cm (8-in) square baking tin (or mould of choice) with non-stick baking spray.

Put the chopped dates in a bowl and cover with the boiling water. Leave for 30 minutes, then mash with a fork and mix in the vanilla.

Mix the flour, baking powder, bicarbonate of soda, cinnamon, ginger and cloves in a bowl and set aside.

In a stand mixer, cream the butter and sugar until pale and fluffy, then add the eggs, one at a time. Add the treacle, then mix in the flour mixture alternating with the milk until everything is combined. Do not overmix. Stir in the date mixture. The mixture will look a bit curdled at this point, but that's fine.

Pour into your prepared tin or mould and bake for 35–40 minutes. Leave to cool in the tin for 10 minutes.

Meanwhile, make the sauce. Combine the butter, sugar, treacle and salt in a medium heavy-based saucepan over a low heat. Mix until fully combined, then add the cream. Turn up the heat until it bubbles and thickens, and you get a nice toffee colour. Remove from the heat.

Unmould the pudding onto a serving plate or cake stand. Cut into squares and drizzle the sauce over it. Serve warm with vanilla ice cream, cream or custard.

# Ginger Bread & Butter Pudding

5–6 Tbsp unsalted butter
10 slices of white bread
Ginger Marmalade (page 114)
1 large egg, plus 4 large egg yolks
3 Tbsp caster (superfine) sugar
500ml (17fl oz/2 cups) double (heavy) cream
200ml (7fl oz/scant 1 cup) whole milk
2 Tbsp demerara (light brown) sugar
1 tsp ground ginger
½ tsp ground cinnamon
¼ tsp freshly grated nutmeg
2 Tbsp flaked (slivered) almonds

This pud is an adaptation of one from goddess of the kitchen Nigella Lawson. In fact, it's an adaptation of her grandmother's recipe, so it is absolutely delicious and warming. If you've never made bread and butter pudding, don't be put off by the idea of covering sandwiches in custard and baking them – it is a delight to eat. I also had my reservations when I first arrived in this country, but I am now truly converted.

*彡*

Preheat the oven to 200°C (180°C fan/400°F/Gas mark 6). Butter a 23cm (9in) baking dish (I normally use a lasagne dish).

Butter all the bread slices, then spoon a couple of tablespoons of the ginger marmalade on five slices of bread and sandwich with the other five. Cut the marmalade sandwiches diagonally into triangles and place them in your prepared dish, overlapping each other with their points facing upwards.

Whisk the egg and egg yolks with the caster sugar in a stand mixer fitted with the whisk attachment. Add the cream and milk, and continue mixing until fully combined.

Pour the eggy mixture over the bread and leave to soak for 5 minutes. Butter the bits of bread poking out of the custard.

Mix the demerara sugar with the ginger, cinnamon and nutmeg, and sprinkle over the pudding.

Bake for 45 minutes, or until the custard has set and puffed up. About 5 minutes before the end of baking, remove the dish from the oven and sprinkle over the flaked almonds.

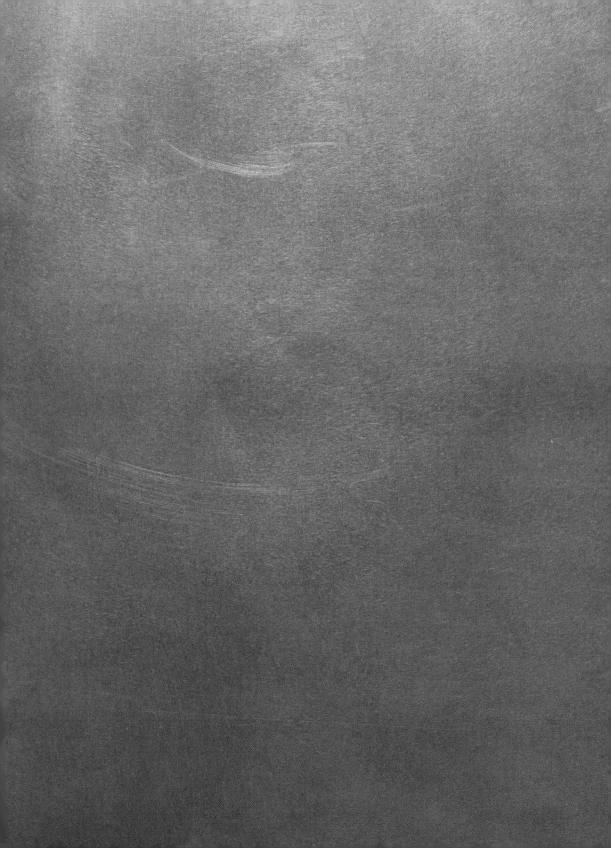

# Drinks

# Gingerbread Latte

120ml (4fl oz/½ cup) freshly
  brewed coffee
1½ Tbsp maple or golden syrup
½ tsp vanilla extract
½ tsp ground ginger
½ tsp ground cinnamon
¼ tsp ground nutmeg
120ml (4fl oz/½ cup) hot milk
whipped cream and freshly
  grated nutmeg to decorate
  (optional)

I have been making my gingerbread latte as long as I have been making my pumpkin spice one, and that's quite a long time. I find ready-made coffee syrups slightly artificial in flavour, so I much prefer to make my own – it takes little effort and it tastes so much better.

In a large mug, combine the hot coffee with the syrup, vanilla and spices, and mix well until dissolved. Pour in the hot milk and mix again.

Serve topped with whipped cream and freshly grated nutmeg.

# Gingerbread Eggnog Cocktail

**FOR THE EGGNOG**

6 medium egg yolks

150g (5 oz/¾ cup) granulated sugar, plus 1 tsp

500ml (17fl oz/2 cups) milk

2 cloves

1 cinnamon stick

225ml (7½fl oz/scant 1 cup) double (heavy) cream

1 tsp freshly grated nutmeg

3–4 Tbsp whisky or bourbon (omit if making it for children)

**FOR THE GINGERBREAD EGGNOG COCKTAIL**

30ml (1fl oz/2 Tbsp) Ginger Syrup (page 123 or from a jar of stem ginger)

30ml (1fl oz/2 Tbsp) rum or whisky

120ml (4fl oz/½ cup) Eggnog ice cubes

**TO DECORATE THE GLASS**

a little extra ginger syrup

crushed ginger biscuits (gingernuts)

Eggnog is synonymous with Christmas in America. Apparently, George Washington used to make his own and was adamant that you should let it rest for a few days to intensify its flavour. I personally love eggnog, on its own, as a latte or in this case as a gingerbread cocktail. Since eggnog is not readily available in the UK, I've included a recipe on how to make it.

∽

Make the eggnog in advance: in a stand mixer fitted with the whisk attachment, whisk the egg yolks with the sugar until light and fluffy.

Combine the milk, cloves and cinnamon stick in a saucepan and heat gently to just before boiling point.

Slowly add about half of the hot milk to the egg mixture, whisking constantly so it doesn't scramble. Pour the mixture back into the saucepan and continue cooking over a low-medium heat until it thickens slightly and coats the back of a wooden spoon. Do not boil. Remove from the heat and leave to cool for 5 minutes.

Stir and strain the mixture through a fine mesh sieve into a bowl. Add the cream, nutmeg and whisky or bourbon, then cover and refrigerate. Leave to 'mature' for 8 hours or overnight.

The eggnog is now ready to serve. You can either ladle it into individual glasses and serve with freshly grated nutmeg and a cinnamon stick, or make the gingerbread cocktail as follows.

To decorate the rim of the glass, pour a little ginger syrup into a saucer and place the crushed ginger biscuits in a separate saucer. Dip the rim of a cocktail glass in the syrup, then dip it into the crushed ginger biscuits to create an attractive rim.

Combine the ginger syrup, the rum or whisky and eggnog in a cocktail shaker filled with ice. Shake well for a few seconds until cold, then strain into your cocktail glass.

# Gingerbread Hot Chocolate

100ml (3½fl oz/7 Tbsp) whole milk
100ml (3½fl oz/7 Tbsp) single (light) cream
1 tsp dark brown sugar
1 tsp orange liqueur (or ½ tsp orange zest)
pinch of salt
pinch of ground ginger
pinch of ground cinnamon
1 whole clove
¼ tsp vanilla extract
50g (1¾oz) dark chocolate, roughly chopped
dollop of whipped cream, sweetened with Ginger Syrup (page 123 or from a jar of stem ginger), to serve (optional)

**This is such a decadent version of a hot chocolate, with hints of ginger, cinnamon and orange. Not one for the kids I'm afraid, although you could substitute the orange liqueur for orange zest.**

Put the milk, cream, sugar, orange liqueur or zest, salt and spices into a medium saucepan set over a low heat. Bring to a gentle simmer while stirring with a wooden spoon. Remove from the heat and leave to infuse for 10 minutes.

If you used orange zest strain the mixture through a sieve, but if you used a liqueur, simply remove the clove. Put the milk back into the pan over a low heat and add the vanilla and chocolate. Stir gently until the chocolate has fully dissolved.

Serve in a mug and top with whipped cream that has been sweetened with ginger syrup, if you like.

# Gingerbread Milkshake

2 stale gingerbread biscuits (or gingernuts/gingersnaps)
1½ scoops vanilla ice cream
120ml (4fl oz/½ cup) whole milk
¼ tsp ground ginger
½ tsp ground cinnamon
whipped cream and crushed gingerbread biscuit, to serve (optional)

There are two ways of making this milkshake. You can make the Gingerbread Gelato (see page 84) and simply blend it with a cup of milk, or you can use vanilla ice cream and add the spices as described below.

Put the gingerbread biscuits into a blender and blitz into crumbs. (Remove 1 teaspoonful if you want some to sprinkle on top of whipped cream to serve.) Add the ice cream, milk and spices and blend until smooth.

Pour into a glass and top with whipped cream and reserved gingerbread crumbs, if using.

# Gingerbread Martini

30ml (1fl oz/2 Tbsp) vodka
60ml (2fl oz/4 Tbsp) Baileys
    Irish Cream liqueur
30ml (1fl oz/2 Tbsp) Ginger
    Syrup (page 123 or from a jar
    of stem ginger)
115ml (3¾fl oz/scant ½ cup)
    single (light) cream or nut
    milk of your choice
1 cup crushed ice

**TO DECORATE THE GLASS**
a little extra ginger syrup
crushed ginger biscuits
    (gingernuts)

I'm not much of an alcohol drinker but I do love a cocktail. This Martini is, for me, the best holiday drink. I even bought a cocktail shaker just to make it.

❧

To decorate the rim of the glass, pour a little ginger syrup into a saucer and place the crushed ginger biscuits in a separate saucer. Dip the rim of a Martini glass in the syrup, then dip it into the crushed ginger biscuits.

Combine all the ingredients in a cocktail shaker and shake for a few seconds, then strain into your glass.

# Gingerbread Black Russian

40ml (1¼fl oz/8 tsp) vodka
20ml (½fl oz/4 tsp) Kahlúa
  coffee liqueur
1½ tsp Ginger Syrup (page 123
  or from a jar of stem ginger)
¼ tsp vanilla extract
ice cubes, plus extra to serve

**A wintry and warming twist on the traditional Black Russian cocktail.**

✦

Pour all the ingredients into a cocktail shaker or a jug filled with ice and shake or muddle until cold.

Strain into a glass filled with extra ice cubes. Skull-shaped ice cube moulds are great for this.

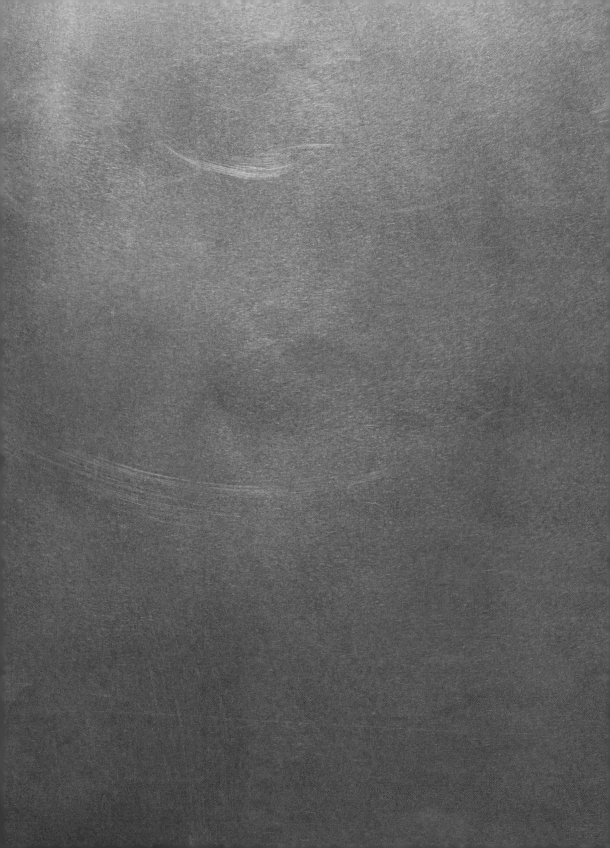

# Gifts from the Kitchen

# Ginger Marmalade

250g (9oz) fresh root ginger
240ml (9fl oz/1 cup) water
150g (5oz/¾ cup) jam sugar
1 Tbsp pectin

**Ginger marmalade is basically an alternative to using stem ginger, and definitely more suitable for spreading on toast or croissants. Use it as you would any other jam.**

Peel the ginger and cut into matchstick strips, then place in a saucepan. Cover with enough water to submerge the ginger, bring to the boil, then simmer for 45 minutes–1 hour. Drain.

Mix the measured water with the jam sugar and pectin in a separate saucepan over a low heat and mix until the sugar is dissolved. Add the ginger strips and simmer for 25–30 minutes.

Pour the marmalade into a sterilized jar, leaving a 1–2cm (½–¾in) space at the top of the jar. Seal with the lid and leave to cool.

Place the jar in a large pan of boiling water, with at least 5cm (2in) of water to cover, and boil for 10 minutes. Remove from the water and leave to cool. While cooling you will hear the lid 'pop' as the vacuum seals. Store in a cool, dark place for up to 12 months. Once opened, keep refrigerated and use within 1 month.

# Homemade Stem Ginger

650g (1lb 7oz) fresh root ginger
1.5 litres (52fl oz/6½ cups)
   water
600g (1lb 5oz/3 cups)
   granulated sugar

Buying stem ginger in shops is rather expensive, so you may want to make it at home. It's simple to make and it tastes better. I have used stem ginger in a few recipes in this book, but it can pretty much be added to any cake, pudding or biscuits. My mother-in-law slices it thinly and has it on toast!

Freeze the ginger overnight.

The next day, remove it from the freezer, peel and slice into 2cm (¾in) slices. Place in a large saucepan and add the measured water (ensure it submerges the ginger by at least 2cm/¾in). Bring to the boil, then simmer for 1½–2 hours until the roots feel tender to the point of a knife.

Drain the ginger, reserving 600ml (21fl oz/generous 2½ cups) of the liquid. Set the ginger aside.

Place the reserved liquid in a separate pan over a medium heat. Add the sugar and stir until it has dissolved, then simmer for about 15 minutes, or until you have a syrup consistency. Add the boiled ginger and continue simmering for a further 15–20 minutes.

Transfer the mixture to a sterilized jar. Seal or store in a cool, dark place for up to 12 months. Once opened, store in the refrigerator for up to 2 months.

# Ginger & Chocolate Honeycomb Coal

2½ tsp bicarbonate of soda
(baking soda)
1 tsp ground ginger
¾ tsp red powder food colour
300g (10½oz/1½ cups) caster
(superfine) sugar
150g (5oz/scant ½ cup) golden
syrup
200g (7oz) dark chocolate,
chopped
200g (7oz/1 cup) black sanding
sugar

Dear Santa, this year I have been rather naughty... You won't mind being on the naughty list this Christmas if this is the kind of coal you'll receive from Santa – homemade honeycomb covered in dark chocolate and sprinkled with black sanding sugar. The honeycomb itself is red, so when you bite into it, it looks like a piece of burning coal.

Line a medium baking tray or a ceramic heatproof dish, about 30 x 20cm (12 x 8in), with baking paper. It helps to grease it first so the paper sticks.

Mix the bicarbonate of soda, ground ginger and the red food colour in a small bowl. If you don't have powder colour, rub gel food colour in with your fingertips until fully combined. Set aside.

Combine the sugar and golden syrup in a heavy-based pan and attach a sugar thermometer to the side. Gently stir over a low heat and try not to let the mixture bubble until completely dissolved. Once the sugar has completely melted, do not stir, to avoid crystallization. Turn the heat up slightly. When the temperature reaches 150°C (300°F), work as quickly as you can to remove the thermometer and tip in the bicarbonate of soda mixture. Gently whisk until the bicarbonate of soda has disappeared and the mixture is foaming. Be careful not to overmix it or you'll lose the bubbles.

Pour the mixture into your prepared tray as close to it as possible, so as not to lose the bubbles. Use a spatula to get it all out of the pan. Leave to cool completely, then crack it into pieces.

Put the chopped chocolate in a heat-resistant bowl and melt in the microwave at 30-second intervals (or melt in a bain marie).

Dip the pieces of honeycomb in the melted chocolate, shaking off the excess (using a fork helps), then cover in the black sanding sugar. Pack in vintage tins and gift to your naughty friends. In my case, all of them!

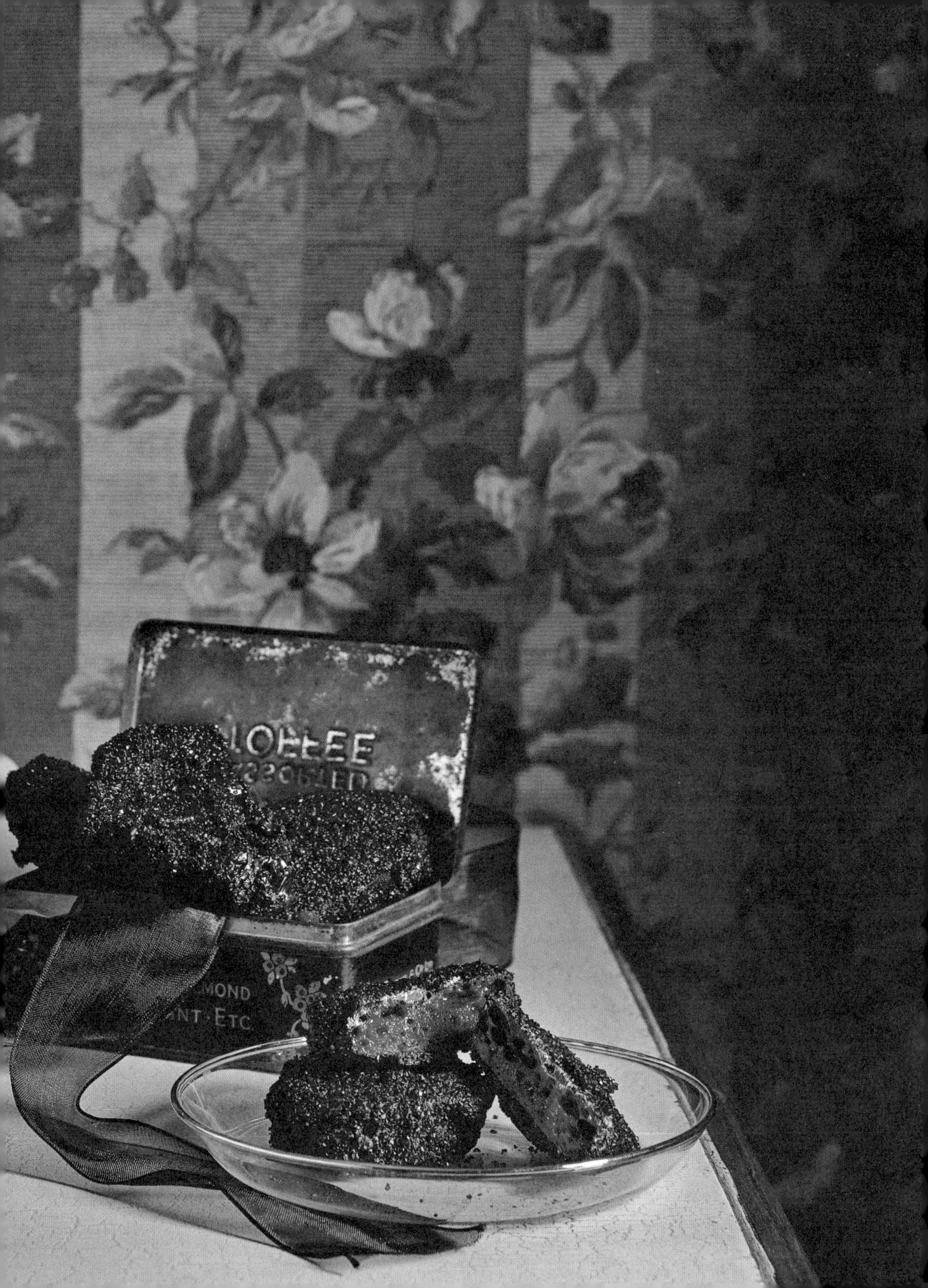

# Pear & Ginger Jam

1.5kg (3lb 5oz) pears, peeled
   and cored
1½ Tbsp grated lemon zest
2 Tbsp grated fresh root ginger
1kg (2lb 4oz/5 cups) granulated
   sugar
1 x 8–10g (¼oz) sachet of
   pectin

Pear and ginger are one of my favourite flavour combinations. Besides using this recipe as a standard jam, you could fill pies or pastries with it. It is also very good combined with almonds. Get some store-bought puff pastry, fill little parcels with the pear and ginger jam, egg wash and bake, then top with flaked (slivered) almonds and icing (confectioners') sugar, for example.

*ellee*

Chop the pears into small cubes and add half to a medium saucepan with enough water to cover the fruit. Bring to the boil, then simmer for about 30 minutes, or until the fruit is soft.

Remove from the heat and add the rest of the pears, lemon zest, ginger, sugar and pectin. Bring back to the boil and continue to boil until it reaches 105°C (220°F) on a sugar thermometer.

Pour the jam into sterilized jars, leaving a 1–2cm (½–¾in) space at the top of the jars. Seal with the lids and leave to cool.

Place the jar in a large pan of boiling water, with at least 5cm (2in) of water to cover, and boil for 10 minutes. Remove from the water and leave to cool. While cooling you will hear the jars 'pop' as the vacuum seals. Store in a cool, dark place for up to 12 months. Once opened, keep refrigerated and use within 1 month.

# Ginger Syrup

200g (7oz/1 cup) granulated sugar
240ml (8fl oz/1 cup) water
115g (4oz) fresh root ginger, peeled and thinly sliced

If you're going to make full use of this recipe book I highly recommend you make your own ginger syrup. It's so simple to prepare and so versatile. I use it in coffee, buttercreams, whipped creams, cocktails, etc. It also makes a lovely gift as part of a gingerbread-themed hamper, or on its own bottled in a festive vessel.

Combine the sugar and water in a medium saucepan set over a medium heat and stir until the sugar has dissolved. Add the ginger and simmer for 30 minutes.

Strain the liquid through a sieve into a jug or bowl and leave it to cool before bottling.

Keep refrigerated for up to 2 weeks.

# Gingerbread Popcorn

100g (3½oz/½ cup) dark brown
  sugar
60g (¼ cup) salted butter
60g (2oz/3 Tbsp) golden or
  maple syrup
1 tsp ground cinnamon
1½ tsp ground ginger
½ tsp salt
1 tsp bicarbonate of soda
  (baking soda)
100g (3½oz/15 cups) freshly
  popped corn (from about
  120g (4oz/⅔ cup) unpopped
  kernels)

**Popcorn is my husband's favourite snack and, although he's all about butter and salt, I have introduced him to this sweet and salty alternative. I love to make this, not just to eat but to give away to loved ones during the holidays. Pack it in glass containers to give it a luxurious touch and finish it off with a ribbon.**

*elle*

Line 2 large baking trays with baking paper or a silicon mat. Set aside.

Combine the sugar, butter, syrup, cinnamon, ginger and salt in a large saucepan over a medium-high heat. Stir until the butter has fully melted and the sugar is dissolved. Bring to the boil while stirring constantly, then add the bicarbonate of soda and mix well.

Remove from the heat and add the popcorn, mixing well so all the popped kernels are covered.

Spread the coated popcorn in a single layer over the trays and leave it to cool completely.

Break the popcorn up and store in an airtight container.

# Mini Yorkshire Parkin Loaves

non-stick baking spray or
  vegetable oil
120g (4¼oz/scant 1 cup) self-
  raising (self-rising) flour
120g (4¼oz/1¼ cups) porridge
  (rolled) oats
1 Tbsp ground ginger
½ tsp salt
90g (6 Tbsp) unsalted butter
120g (4¼oz/6 Tbsp) golden
  syrup
40g (1½oz/2 Tbsp) black treacle
90g (3¼oz/scant ½ cup) soft
  brown sugar
1 medium egg, plus 1 egg yolk
130ml (4½fl oz/generous
  ½ cup) whole milk
½ tsp bicarbonate of soda
  (baking soda)

If you have read the very brief history of gingerbread at the beginning
of this book, you already know what Yorkshire parkin is and that it is
traditionally eaten on Bonfire Night. Parkin is perfect to give as a gift,
as it stays fresh for way longer than most cakes. In fact, it is best eaten
two or three days after baking. I have used some decorative autumnal
mini loaf tins to make it extra pretty, but you can just bake it in a
20-cm (8-in) square baking tin and cut it into squares.

ﻌﻌﻌﻌﻌ

Preheat the oven to 195°C (175°C fan/375°F/Gas mark 5). Spray
the tin/s you are using to bake the parkin with non-stick baking spray
or brush with vegetable oil.

Mix the flour, oats, ginger and salt in a large bowl with a whisk and
set aside.

Combine the butter, syrup, treacle and sugar in a medium saucepan
set over a medium-low heat and stir until the butter has melted and
everything is combined. Pour the hot mixture over the dry ingredients.

Beat the egg and egg yolk in a jug, add the milk while still beating and
then add the bicarbonate of soda. Pour this over the flour/syrup mixture
and combine well.

Pour the batter into your prepared tin/s and bake: 30–35 minutes
if baking in one large tin; 25–30 minutes if using individual tins.

Let the parkin cool before removing from the tins. It will stay fresh
for around 10 days.

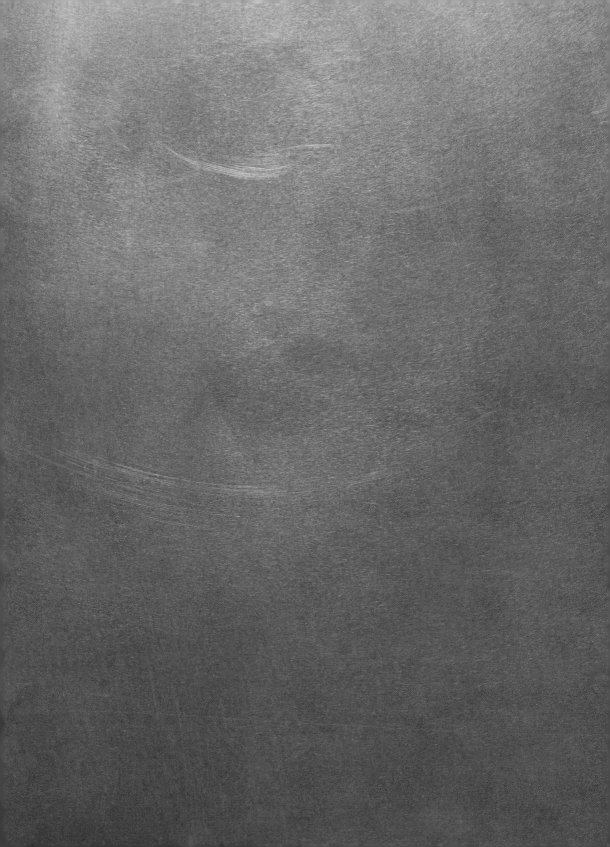

# Gingerbread Houses

This chapter might be more accurately named 'Gingerbread Structures'. I've made a Romany wagon, a Tudor pub, a Ouija board and Baba Yaga's hut out of gingerbread. The templates are all provided at the end of this book – you can scan them and adjust the sizes, if you wish.

I'd like to give you a few tips to help you succeed when making a gingerbread structure:

First, they take effort, so spread the work over several days, making the dough and baking on one day, decorating on another day, and assembling on a third day, for example.

Refrigerate the cut-out shapes while on their trays before baking.

It is always better to slightly overbake the biscuit than underbake it for these projects.

A fine grater will help you get edges straight before assembling.

If you are planning to eat the gingerbread house, use caramel as glue, as it dries much faster than royal icing. However, if you are not planning to eat it and just making it to display over the holidays, get the glue gun out! It works wonders with gingerbread.

I recommend using remote-control fairy lights, so you can turn them on and off without having to lift anything and risk destroying what took you days to make.

Don't be put off by the work involved or think they require skills you do not possess. The Romany wagon was the first gingerbread structure I ever made and making the templates was probably the hardest bit, thankfully they're available for you at the end of this book. If you put your mind to it, you can achieve anything.

# Gingerbread Romany Vardo Wagon

2 x batches Basic
  Gingerbread Dough
  (page 46)
1 x batch Royal Icing
  (page 47)
200g (7oz) white fondant
turquoise food colour
green food colour
red food colour
black edible paint
gold edible paint
red ball sprinkles

If you follow me on Instagram, you may have noticed that last year I bought an adorable Romany wagon for my garden. It is my pride and joy. Just as I do in my home, I dress it up for the seasons. Beautiful fresh flowers surround it in the spring and summer, pumpkins and lanterns in the autumn and Christmas lights, wreaths and garlands in the winter. This is how to make the gingerbread version.

I made the template for this wagon using a postage tube, 11cm (4¼in) in diameter. Although there are templates for you to print and cut out on pages 146–147, you will still need the tube shape for the baking stage.

*℮ℓℓ℮*

Make the gingerbread dough according to the instructions on page 46.

After rolling the dough out, cut around the templates provided on pages 146–147. For the roof section, cut out a rectangular piece of dough to match the length of the base panel. For the width, measure the curve of the front and back panels and match that measurement. Place the shapes on baking trays lined with baking paper. For the roof section, cover a section of your postage tube with foil and drape the gingerbread over it before placing on the baking tray.

Bake for 15–18 minutes. Allow to cool completely before decorating.

Decorate the front and back panels with coloured fondant and royal icing. You can copy the designs I've made, but feel free to colour and paint in whichever way you please.

Paint around the wheel edges with black edible paint to imitate tyres. Pipe in the spokes with royal icing and paint them with gold edible paint when dry.

PLEASE
TURN OVER

When all the bits that need decorating have dried, it's time to assemble. Use royal icing to glue the front and back panels of the caravan to the base. Use something to prop them up while they dry (a tin can works well). Next, glue on the side panels. Let everything dry before attaching the roof.

Once the roof is secured, cover with a rectangle of turquoise-coloured fondant. Brush it with a little water so it sticks.

Prop up the base of the caravan on a tin (can) of sardines, or similar, and attach the wheels to the sides and the steps to the front. Leave to dry, then pipe a little royal icing foliage dotted with red ball sprinkles to cover up the fondant edges.

# Gingerbread Pub

2–3 x batches Basic
  Gingerbread Dough
  (page 46)
2 x batches Royal Icing
  (page 47)
4 gelatine leaves
caramel or isomalt, for
  glueing
small battery-powered wire
  fairy lights (optional)
500g (1lb 2oz) black fondant
50g (1¾oz) brown fondant
lollipop stick and coloured
  string for the pub sign
green gel food colour
edible pearls

**Who doesn't love a traditional old British pub decked out for the holidays with a roaring fire? For this project, I wanted to go for a Tudor-style two-storey building. I imagine it to be full of drunken revellers, singing, hitting their heads on the low ceiling beams and dropping their pints of ale.**

Make the gingerbread dough according to the instructions on page 46.

After rolling the dough out, cut around the templates provided on pages 148–151. For the bottom storey of the pub, use the long sides of the top storey from page 151 and the short sides of the top storey from page 149, minus the triangular top. Place on a baking tray lined with baking paper.

Bake for 12–15 minutes. Allow to cool completely before decorating.

Use a little royal icing to attach the gelatine leaves behind all the window openings. Leave to dry.

Assemble both storeys of the pub separately using caramel or isomalt as glue. Melt the caramel or isomalt in a large, wide frying pan (skillet), so you have room to dip the walls of the pub into it. Reheat when necessary. If you are using fairy lights to illuminate your pub, make sure you put them in before the roof goes on and have access to the on/off switch.

To make the roof tiles, cut out long strips of back fondant and make small incisions along the length of each strip to look like tiles. Mount each strip overlapping each other, glueing them to the roof with royal icing, starting at the bottom and working your way up.

Ice the walls of of both structures with royal icing. Before it dries, decorate with beams made out of strips of black fondant. The design is up to you.

PLEASE
TURN OVER

135

I made the pub door using a silicon mould, but you can cut strips of brown fondant, score them with a modelling tool to make them look like wood and place them next to each other to form a door shape. Make the hinges and doorknob out of black fondant.

Insert the lollipop stick for the pub sign and secure it with a little melted caramel. Decorate your pub sign as you wish and hang it from the lollipop stick with some coloured string.

Before you attach the top storey of the pub to the bottom, place a tin can in the middle of the bottom structure for extra support before you place the top storey.

Colour some royal icing in green and pipe some leaves around the front and sides to create Christmas garlands. Decorate with edible pearls. Add finishing touches by piping a little royal icing snow along the tops of the windows and roof ridge. I didn't do this, but some little fairy lights around the outside of the roof would also look adorable.

# Gingerbread Baba Yaga Hut

1½ batches Basic Gingerbread Dough (page 46)
250g (9oz) modelling chocolate (you could also use fondant but modelling chocolate hardens better)
250g (9oz) dark chocolate, grated
Royal Icing (page 47)
brown food colour
caramel or isomalt, for glueing

If you haven't heard of Baba Yaga before, she – along with her two sisters – is a fascinating character in Slavic folklore. Described as a ferocious-looking witch or ogress, she travels by mortar holding a pestle. As with many fairytale witches, Baba Yaga is capable of good and evil. She lives deep in the forest in a hut described that can walk because it has chicken legs. I could not resist making her hut out of gingerbread for this book.

You'll need to make a simple wooden platform from plywood, with two wooden rods that will be covered with modelling chocolate to make the chicken feet.

*ellle*

For the platform, you need a piece of 6-mm (¼-in) thick ply, cut to form a 10cm (6in) by (7in) base. Screw into this two 15-cm (6-in) long wooden rods or dowelling to form the chicken legs. Cover the rods in modelling chocolate and sculpt the chicken feet then stand the rods on a board, supported under the platform by tin cans, and allow the chocolate to set. It helps to use a picture of real chicken legs as reference.

Make the gingerbread dough according to the instructions on page 46. After rolling the dough out, cut around the templates provided on pages 149–151 for the sides and roof, and page 148 for the chimney. The door and window can be either moulded by hand or you can use silicon moulds. Before you bake all elements, use a sharp knife to slightly curve the roof and wall sides by cutting at an angle. Bake for 12–15 minutes. Allow to cool completely before decorating. Attach the door and windows and any decorations to the front wall panel with a little royal icing.

Brush some brown coloured royal icing at the top of the front wall and all over the roof pieces and cover with the grated chocolate. Or alternatively cover all walls and roof in grated chocolate like I did. Assemble all pieces on top of the wooden platform using caramel to stick them together (or a glue gun if you're not planning on eating the hut). Finally brush some more royal icing at the bottom of the hut to hide the wooden platform.

# Ouija Board

1 batch Basic Gingerbread
  Dough (page 46)
black food paint
isomalt, for glueing
Royal Icing (page 47 –
  optional)

This Ouija board is probably the simplest of the gingerbread structures in this book but it looks just great. Once you summon the spirits you can simply eat the whole thing. I bought an A4 template for the letters and numbers, however you can print the one I made for *The Witch-crafting Handbook* on pages 152–153 and cut the letters/numbers out. I added a little keyhole detail to the planchette and a key to the board simply because I already had those moulds and to me they represented opening the door to another dimension. This isn't necessary at all; you can paint your design or add other gingerbread bits.

*ellee*

Make the gingerbread dough according to the instructions on page 46.

After rolling the dough out, cut around the templates provided on pages 154–155 and bake.

Place the letters and numbers template on top of the Ouija board and dab a little edible paint onto a piece of sponge. Apply carefully to cover all. Let the paint dry and then remove the template.

Using a thin brush, draw a black line all around the board and planchette to give a little more definition.

Attach any other gingerbread decorations (in my case key/keyhole) with a little edible glue or royal icing.

To make the little isomalt 'glass' piece for the planchette there are different methods you can use. The easiest would be just to melt the isomalt in the microwave and pour a bit into the hole, making sure it's placed on parchment paper or a silicon mat. To make it oval, however, you could pour a thin layer over a small semi-circle silicon mould that's turned upside down. I used the third method which is to pour the melted isomalt onto clingfilm (plastic wrap) and apply pressure around it with a metal ring. This is a technique developed by pastry wizard Amaury Guichon.

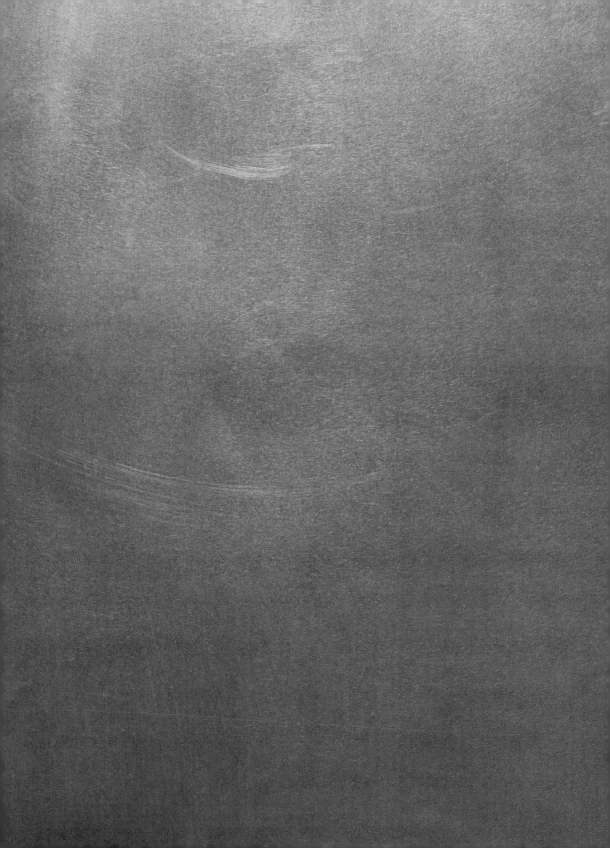

# Templates

# Demogorgon Template

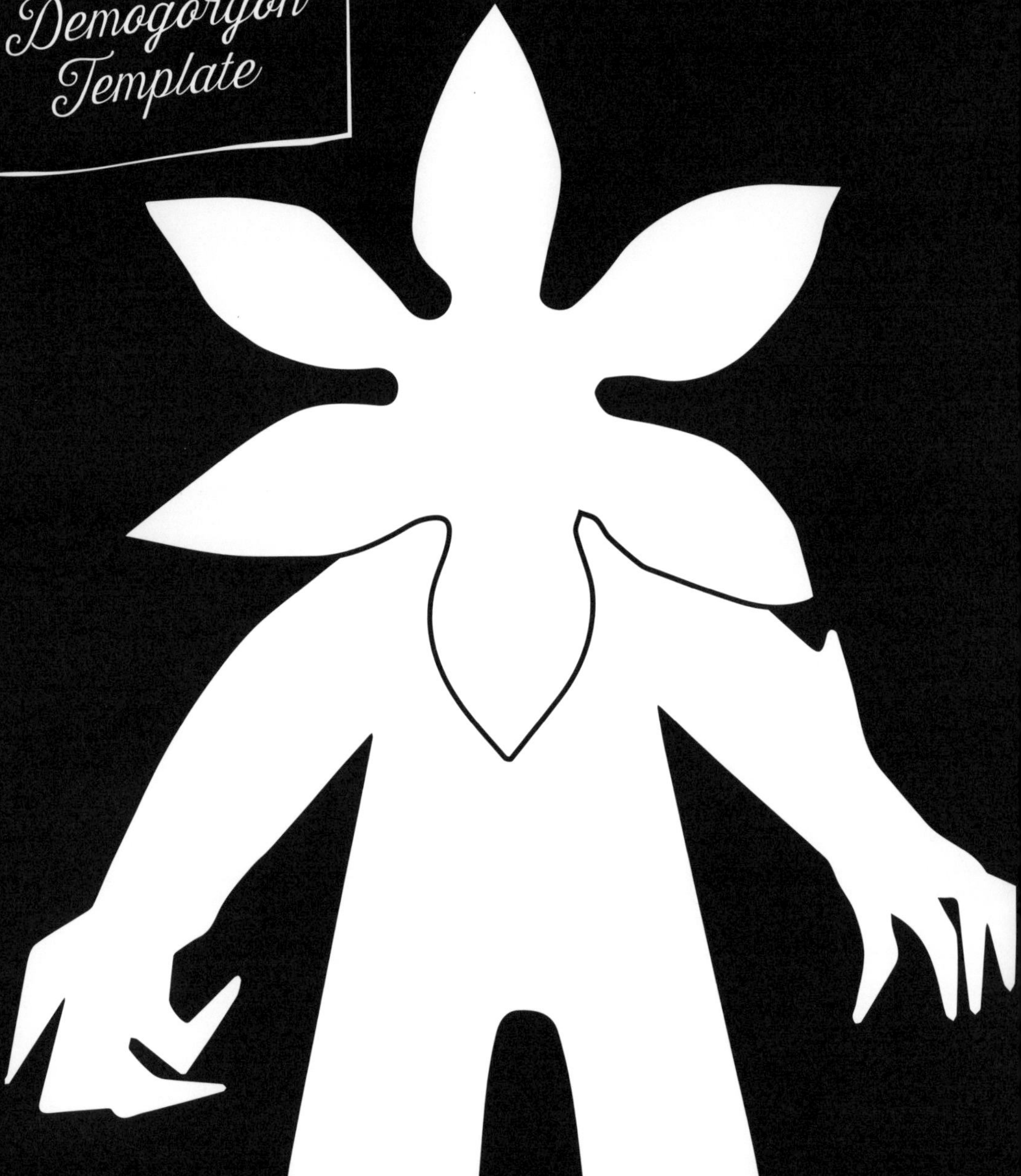

# Dome Cake Template

STRAWBERRY

CHOCOLATE

12cm/4.7"

VANILLA

SPONGE

11.5cm/4.5"

# Gingerbread Romany Vardo Wagon Template

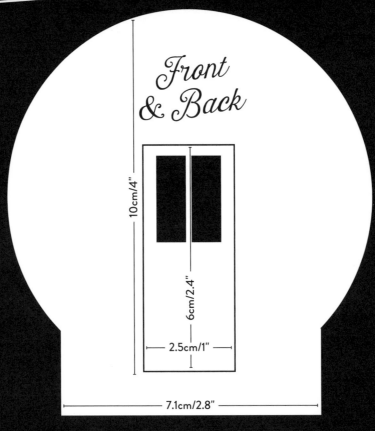

Front & Back

10cm/4"

6cm/2.4"

2.5cm/1"

7.1cm/2.8"

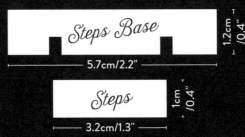

Steps Base

1.2cm /0.4"

5.7cm/2.2"

Steps

1cm /0.4"

3.2cm/1.3"

Bottom

16cm/6.3"

7.5cm/3"

Sides x 2

12.5cm/5"

1.5cm
/0.6"

# Gingerbread Pub Template

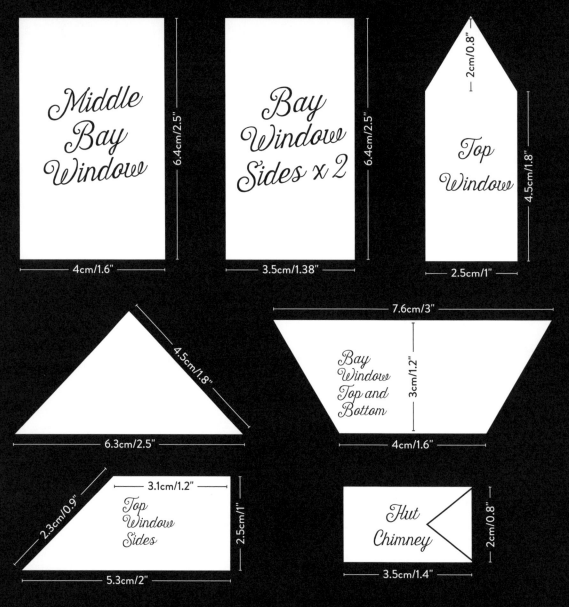

Middle Bay Window — 6.4cm/2.5" — 4cm/1.6"

Bay Window Sides x 2 — 6.4cm/2.5" — 3.5cm/1.38"

Top Window — 2cm/0.8" — 4.5cm/1.8" — 2.5cm/1"

4.5cm/1.8" — 6.3cm/2.5"

Bay Window Top and Bottom — 7.6cm/3" — 3cm/1.2" — 4cm/1.6"

Top Window Sides — 3.1cm/1.2" — 2.3cm/0.9" — 2.5cm/1" — 5.3cm/2"

Hut Chimney — 2cm/0.8" — 3.5cm/1.4"

11.3cm/4.5"

8.3cm/3.3"

12.7cm/5"

*Front and Back Top
(use for bottom storey
sides without the
triangular top)*

15.2cm/6"

Roof top x 2

17.8cm/7"

*Sides top x 2 and bottom storey x 2*

12.7cm/5"

A B C D E F G
N O P Q R S T
1 2 3 4 5

# HIJKLM
## UVWXYZ

# 67890

21cm/8.3"

29.7cm/11.7"

# Index

# Acknowledgements

Thank you to all who made this book possible. First, to Sarah from Quadrille who put
the idea forward – it ended up being a wonderful book to write. To Sophie, Claire
and Georgie for their patience and input. To Patsy for once again photographing
the bakes beautifully and Sam for his invaluable assistance. To Agathe for her
stunning propping and the lovely Katie for her huge help in the kitchen. And last,
but certainly not least, to my agent Vivienne and my friends and family for always
cheering me on.

*Helena Garcia* was inspired by her first experience of Halloween whilst
living in Las Vegas, and quickly became hooked on all things gothic and quirky,
a passion that infused her bakes when she competed in the *Great British Bake*
*Off* 2019, with her eccentric style and fun-loving personality making her an
exceptionally popular contestant. Having run a beautiful Victorian apothecary
in Leeds, Helena infuses her stylish, spooky approach into everything she creates,
including the sell-out merchandise available on her website. She is the author
of *The Wicked Baker* (2020) and *The Witch-Crafting Handbook* (2021).
witchesbyhelenagarcia.com
@helenagarciafp

# Dedication

'To my family, and that includes my dog of course!'

**Managing Director** Sarah Lavelle
**Designer** Georgie Hewitt
**Photographer** Patricia Niven
**Food Stylist** Katie Marshall
**Props Stylist** Agathe Gits
**Production Director** Stephen Lang
**Production Controller** Sabeena Atchia

Published in 2023 by Quadrille, an imprint of Hardie Grant Publishing

**Quadrille**
52–54 Southwark Street
London SE1 1UN
quadrille.com

Cataloguing in Publication Data: a catalogue record for this book is available from
the British Library.

Text © Helena Garcia 2023
Photography © Patricia Niven 2023
Design © Quadrille 2023

ISBN 978 1 83783 0411

Printed in China